Jicarilla Apache Texts

The Traditions, Stories, Legends and Myths of the Apache Native American Jicarilla Tribes

By Pliny Earle Goddard

PANTIANOS
CLASSICS

Published by Pantianos Classics

ISBN-13: 978-1-78987-142-5

First published in 1911

Contents

Introduction

The Jicarilla Apache, at the time of the American occupation of New Mexico and Arizona, were living in two bands. One of these, generally called the Llanero, made their homes in the mountains between the Rio Grande and the Plains. The second band, known as the Ollero, lived along the Chama River, west of the Rio Grande. For several decades the first-mentioned band was cared for by Indian agents at Cimarron and Taos, while the Ollero received rations at Abiquiu. In 1880 both bands were taken to Tierra Amarilla but in 1884 were removed to the Mescalero Reservation. In 1887 they were finally placed where they are now living on a reservation in northern New Mexico on the headwaters of the San Juan River. They now number 776.

They have been politically associated with the Southern Ute to whom they appear to be very closely related in matters of material culture. The relation of the Jicarilla with the inhabitants of Taos seems not to have been so intimate. They occupied the territory surrounding the pueblo of Taos, either with or without the consent of its inhabitants, but were not allowed to remain in the pueblo over night or to witness important ceremonies. Their relations with the Indians of the Plains seem to have been perpetually hostile. They grouped them under the name of Inda and seemed not to have known them by their usual tribal names. At least in recent times, they have looked upon the Navajo as their enemies. The Navajo were obliged to pass through the territory of the Ute and Jicarilla in order to reach the buffalo upon the Plains. Such journeys were accomplished at night according to the usual custom in passing through the territory of an enemy.

The method of life of the Jicarilla seems to have been very similar to that of the Plains Indians. They used skin tipis and depended mostly upon buffalo and smaller game for their food supply. They seem to have planted corn only to a limited extent.

In language, they belong to the southern division of the Athapascan stock. Taken as a whole, the languages of the southern division have a definite unity as compared with the Athapascan languages on the Pacific Coast and in the Far North. This unity is marked by a considerable proportion of words, even of stems, peculiar to the southern division, and also by certain phonetic shifts. While there is considerable diversity within the southern division, the speaker of any one dialect seems to be understood by speakers of all the others. The greatest difficulty probably would be in the case of a Navajo speaking with a Lipan. The most definite sub-group in this division is occasioned by the regular shift of the strongly aspirated t, to an equally aspirated k. This shift has taken place in the Lipan, Jicarilla, and Kiowa-Apache. It is expected that the material here presented in the form of texts will form the basis for a grammatical study of the Jicarilla. When similar material has been published for the Kiowa-Apache, Mescalero and San Carlos Apache a comparative grammar of the southern division will be possible.

The Southern Athapascan peoples, except the Kiowa-Apache, seem to share in a common mythology. It is chiefly characterized by a divine woman who becomes the mother or grandmother of one or two culture heroes. One of these is thought to be the son of the sun and the other one, the descendant of the water. They make a visit to the sun to secure supernatural power and efficient weapons with which they rid the world of most of its evils. The accounts from the different peoples of this area agree rather closely in the incidents and details related and in the names of the characters. Those of the Jicarilla alone, show any definite, close connection with similar culture heroes believed in by the Blackfoot, Shoshone, and other peoples of the north. The Southern Athapascan also have a common belief in gods thought to inhabit the numerous ruins or to live in the interior of mountains. With these gods are connected many of their ceremonies. There is throughout the area considerable agreement as to the personal names of these gods.

The narratives of the second group here presented are mostly coyote stories many of which are not peculiar to the Southwest but are found to the north among the Shoshone of the Plateaus and the Blackfoot of the Plains. A considerable number of traditional narratives and personal experiences has been presented because many of these illustrate customs and methods prevailing in war and the chase. Descriptions of ceremonies and of processes employed in preparing food, etc., have also been given in the form of texts.

The larger number of texts was secured from Casa Maria, a Jicarilla now about seventy years of age and nearly blind. He knows an unusual number and variety of tales and myths, has an excellent memory, and unusual patience. His enunciation was unusually distinct. A few texts, indicated in footnotes, were obtained from Juan Pesita. These were the first recorded and are much less perfect in form, due partly to the lack of familiarity with the language on the part of the recorder. These texts, however, were phonetically verified by means of the Rousselot phonetic apparatus. This was of particular aid in distinguishing the three series of stops and the occurrence of glottal stops and catches. Probably the most serious phonetic defect in the texts is that of the nasalized vowels. To the natural difficulty in hearing by one whose attention has not been trained by the use of a language where nasalization is associated with a difference in meaning is to be added the effect of habit, soon acquired, of writing each syllable or word in one manner, regardless of minor variations.

Reuben Springer, a Jicarilla, served as interpreter it the time the texts were recorded. Thanks are due Edward Ladd for assistance both with the text of the Jicarilla and the interlinear translations while the paper was in proof.

The Jicarilla first received the attention of Mr. James Mooney in 1897 resulting in a publication, The Jicarilla Genesis, in the 11th volume of the American Anthropologist old series. Dr. Frank Russell collected a number of myths and tales published under the title of "Myths of the Jicarilla Apache," in the 11th volume of the Journal of American Folk-Lore. The material here presented was obtained during the months of August, September, and October, 1909, under the direction of the Appointive Committee on the Southwest of which Mr. Archer M. Huntington is the chairman.

August, 1911.

1. The Emergence

In the beginning, the people were coming up. He [2] made a mountain that continued to increase in height. Then he caused reeds to stand vertically in the center. The people were gathered about the mountain, watching. When the reeds were approaching the sky, four girls went up the mountain and twisted them. They went down and left them in this condition. The people tried in vain to make the reeds grow. "Go up and see what has happened to them," he told someone. This person, on ascending the mountain, found the reeds were twisted and that those who had done it had gone down. The messenger, when he came down, said, "The reeds are twisted."

Then four ladders were made and placed in position: [3] one black, one blue, one yellow, and one variegated. Then whirlwind went to the world above and looked. When he came back he reported that there was much water there. [4]

After a time, the one in charge, told Beaver to go and see how conditions were. When Beaver got to the upper world, he found the water receding and commenced piling dirt in front of it to retain it. When Beaver did not return, Badger was told to go after him and see what had happened. He found Beaver building a dam in front of the water. "When the people come up and the children are dying of thirst, they will drink this," said Beaver in explanation of his conduct. Badger went into the mud (producing certain markings). The two went down and reported that the land was already exposed.

The people prepared to ascend. The black ladder was placed in position and the people went up by means of it until it was worn out. The blue ladder was next put in place. When it was worn out the yellow ladder was put up. By the time it was worn out nearly all the people had gone up. Last of all, the variegated ladder was placed in position. When the last of the people had gone up it, too, was worn out. There remained behind a feeble old woman and an old man. The people went away and left them sitting there. "Take us out," one of them called after them. The people stopped and looked back at the couple but did not take them out. Then one of them said, "You will come back here to me." [5]

Then the people moved away towards the east along four parallel trails under four chiefs. Those who went by the first road had fighting. Those going along the second road were fortunate and came back without having had a fight. The people who had gone by the third road, having had a fight, returned. The fourth man came back without having had any trouble. The leadership of the chief of the first band was unfortunate, that of the second band fortunate, that of the third band unfortunate, and that of the fourth band fortunate. They moved back to their own country near Taos.

[1] This account is much abbreviated, Mooney's version speaks of four mountains of the four colors; and explains that the girls were picking berries and flowers and that their mere presence caused the mountains to stop growing. He mentions, Polecat, Crow (Raven), in addition to Beaver and Badger as messengers sent. In each case peculiar markings resulted. Mooney, (a). p. 197.

Russell tells that the mountains grew during four nights; that the girls who caused them to stop growing became rabbits; that Badger and Turkey were the messengers; that the whirlwind dried up the water; and that one old woman remained behind from choice. Russell, (a), p. 254.

Compare also, Matthews, pp. 63-76; Franciscan Fathers, pp. 351-2.

[2] The person who did this was Xastc'iniLgaiyîn, White god of the east, assisted by Xastc'inyaLkîdn, Talking god of the south, Xastc'inîLtsôyin, Yellow god of the west, and Xaste'inîdlôyin, Laughing god of the north. This was the order in which they were mentioned. It is usual to associate Xastc'inyaLkîdn with the east. Cf. p. 265.

[3] It was explained that two of the ladders were made of elkhorns with four horns on each side for rails and separate horns for the, rounds. The other two ladders were of buffalo horn.

The continual reoccurrence of the number four, the objects or incidents being usually associated with the cardinal points and their appropriate colors is characteristic of the myths and ceremonies of the southern Athapascan.

[4] Black Whirlwind caused the water to dry up.

[5] These two are the rulers of the world of the dead which the ghosts reached through the place of emergence. They pass down easily but cannot return because the ladders are worn out. This place is said to be situated somewhere many miles north of Taos and is reached by four trails. Compare, Russell, (a), p. 255.

The Navajo tell of the death of a hermaphrodite twin afterward seen sitting in the lower world who became the ruler of the ghosts, Matthews, p. 77 and note 50.

2. The First War

Raven divined to see whether people would die. First, he threw in the stick over which the skins are stretched in dressing. When this came to the top of the water he tried again by throwing the stone muller. It did not come to the surface and the people began to die. [1]

The people moved away in four directions but they could not sleep. The old couple of the lower world to whom they came back gave them four lice, two of which were placed in their hair, and two in their clothes., When they lay down they were all very sleepy. It was the biting of the lice that made them sleep. [2]

Some of the people occupied the country near the head of the Arkansas River; others, were living along the Sangro de Cristo Range; and the remainder on the west side of the Rio Grande. There were two chiefs of those on the east side of the river named, Indayedittsitdn, and IndakadigaLn. The first named chief made a corral and gave a feast to which he invited all the people. IndakadigaLn, alone, of all the people, refused to attend. After being repeatedly called by name, he finally came, holding an arrow in place on his stretched bow, saying, "Why did you call my name?" "I did not call it for any particular purpose," the other replied. "I thought you called it for some reason," said the first, from whom the people were going away, because he was making motions as if to shoot. He shot an arrow to the feathers through Indayedittsitdn's arm and then went home.

The wounded chief sent word to the one who had shot him asking him to come quickly and take the arrow out. When he refused, he sent to him again, saving "Hurry, come and take the arrow out." Neither this, nor a third message to the same effect, had any result. The fourth time he instructed the messenger to say, "Do not be afraid, come to me, and bring some medicine." Then IndakadigaLn quickly took up his medicine bag, looked inside, and selected the required herb. When he came to the wounded man he found the arm badly swollen. "My grandchild, I did not intend to shoot you." He then cut into the outside of the arm, took out the arrow, and applied the medicine. "The swelling will be gone in four days," he told him. He was well in four days and became the grandson of the chief who had shot him.

Having moved the camp to the east side of the river, IndakadigaLdn, brought together five hundred men and started away to fight with the enemy. He took along ten horses for his own use in battle. When they came to the enemy and were surrounded by them, the chief said, "Wait until tomorrow and you will have some fun. Keep away from me." The next morning, the chief said, "Now, we are ready." There were many arrows ready for his use. He selected four men, who, remaining out of the battle, should carry home the report of the outcome.

"Who is chief?" asked one of the enemy. "I am the only chief," replied IndakadigaLdn. "Who is your chief?" he asked of the enemy. There were four chiefs of the enemy. IndakadigaLdn rode his horse toward the enemy and commenced the fighting. A number of men were killed on both sides. When the chief's horse was killed under him, he jumped on another and continued fighting. He continued to do this as his people decreased in numbers until five horses had been killed under him. When he had mounted the sixth horse and his people had all been killed the enemy pulled him to the ground and killed him with a knife.

The four men who had been selected for the purpose went back to their country and reported, "Our people are all dead." When Indayedittsitdn had received the message he cut off his hair saying, "My grandson has been killed, I will mourn for him properly."

[1] Russell has this incident as a variant, (a), p. 255. The Navajo account has Coyote instead of Raven as the diviner, Matthews, p. 77. Compare also, Wissler and Duvall, p. 20; Dorsey and Kroeber, p. 17.

[2] Russell, (a), p. 255.

3. The Culture Heroes and Owl

[1]
Kubatc'istcine and Naiyenesgani were companions. When they came to visit their grandmother, YoLgaiistdzan [2] they said to her, "Make us something to play with." "Go and see your father," she replied. When they came near the house of the sun, children put their heads out of the door and looked at them. When their mother was told who was coining, she said to her husband, "You always claim that you do nothing wrong and here are your children, coming to see you." "Come in and sit back of the fire," they were told when they arrived. "Why did you come to see me?" asked the sun. "We want something to play with," they replied. He made the hoop and pole game and some arrows for them. "You must not roll the hoop toward the north," he told them.

They went about playing with the hoop and poles. After some time, they rolled it to the north. Although they threw the poles after the hoop it rolled straight on, without falling, into the house of Owl and fell back of the fire. When Owl saw the two boys standing there, he said, sort of people have come to see me? Hurry up and put them in the pot to cook." Kubatc'istcine said, "I am stronger than he." Owl's wife chopped them up, put them in a pot, poured water over them, and put them by the fire to boil. Although the water was boiling, they stood in the bottom of the pot, telling stories to each other. "Well, take them up for me," said Owl, "I want something to eat." His wife poked a stick into the pot and one of the boys jumped out to one side. She put the stick in again and the other one jumped out. Owl looked at them and said, "You are something bad, you are using supernatural power so that you may not die."

The boys were still standing there. "Hurry, put them in the ashes to roast for me," Owl said. Naiyenesgani said, "I am stronger than he." Then she separated the ashes, put them in the middle of the fire, and arranged the fire on top of them, They sat there in the middle of the fire telling stories. [3]

"Hurry now, I want to eat," he said, "take them out for me." When she poked in the ashes for them, one of them jumped out. Then she poked again and the other jumped out. "Why did you come here practising magic?" Owl said, "Give them the hoop and pole," he told someone. They were given to them. "Go right around the hill here," Owl said.

The two boys started off and came again to their father. "I told you not to roll it in that direction," he said to them. They went back to their grandmother. "See here, our father made us something nice to play with," they said. They went around playing with it until sunset.

[1] Mooney, (a), p. 201; compare also, Lowie, (a), p. 281.

13

[2] There are many varying versions as to the origin of these gods or culture among the several Apache tribes and the Navajo. Some insist that there is but one person with two names. Those who hold that there are two persons say that water is the father of Kubatc'istcine and that the sun is the father of Naiyenesgani. It is sometimes said that Isdzanadlehe is the mother of both. Others say that their mothers are sisters, or mother and daughter. In nearly all cases, regardless of the relationship assumed, they both address the woman as grandmother.

These culture heroes in the details of their names, birth, and exploits, are Southwestern in only a few particulars are they clearly connected with the twin brothers of northern mythology (Lowie, (a), pp. 280-7; Wissler and Duvall, pp. 40-53.) Dr. Lowie has fully discussed the distribution of this and related myths, (b), pp. 97-148.

[3] The Kiowa-Apache, who have this myth, explain that one being, the son of the water was able to protect himself in the pot, and the other could not be hurt by fire. The Kiowa-Apache names are different.

4. The Killing of The Monsters

Naiyenesgani came where Elk had been killing people. He could not get near it although he tried to approach it from every side. Then another person came to him to be his partner. "My companion," he said, "I will gnaw off the hair on his breast for you." Having done this he returned, saying, "Now go to him."

Naiyenesgani went to him, made motions four times, and then shot him. He hid in one of the holes that his partner had made. The elk broke out the uppermost hole. Naiyenesgani went into the next hole. The elk broke that out also. He then went into mother which Elk also broke out.

He went into the bottom tunnel; just as Elk broke this out he fell down dead. The partner then came up to him and said, "The breast will be mine." Naiyenesgani skinned it and took the hide. He also chopped off one of the horns. He filled two of the blood vessels with blood and spread out the hide in the sun until it was dry. [1]

He started away toward the eagle. 2 When he came to him he wrapped the elk hide about himself and went out into an open place. The eagle, when he swooped down, attempted to drive his talons into him but could not penetrate the hide. He flew up without getting hold of him. He came to him again but failed to get his talons in. He flew up again. He came back and having failed, flew away again. Then he came back and drove in his talons. He flew away to his home with the man. He brought him to his young. When they bent their heads down over him he said, "Sst." "Father, when we put our heads down to it, it says 'sst,'" one of them said. "Do not mind it; go ahead and eat. It is the air coming out of the wound that makes that noise." Then the blood flowed through the opening. The old eagle flew away.

Naiyenesgani came up to them holding the horn in his hand. "When your father comes home, on what rock does he sit?" he asked. "He sits on yonder point of rock," one of them told him. Naiyenesgani sat there with eagle's children until the father came again bringing with him a pretty dead girl which he threw down. Making motions four times, Naiyenesgani struck him and he fell into the canyon. He heard him burst as he struck. "When your mother comes back, where does she sit?" he asked. "She sit, here," one of them said. The mother came back. Naiyenesgani making motions four times, struck her, throwing her into the canyon. Then he said to the young eagles, "You will be just as large as you are now. People will like your feathers." "Those who take them will have their muscles draw up." "You shall not talk," he said. Then they ceased talking.

In the distance, his grandmother (bat) was coming into the open from the timber. She walked along carrying a basket. Then he shouted to her, "Grandmother, take me down," but she did not hear. He shouted to her again and then she heard. Then his grandmother came near him. "I shouted to you, 'take me down, grandmother,'" he said. "Come up to me and take me down," he told her. Then she climbed up to him, carrying her basket. "Grandmother, this carrying rope on your basket is very small." "Why, grandson, I carry very heavy things with this. Fill it with stones and see if it breaks." When he had filled it she jumped with it. Then she took the stones out again and he got in. "Shut your grandson." She started to go down with him. "Do not open your eyes, eyes, grandson," she cautioned him, the rock is sheer. We are falling, grandson, do not open your eyes. We are down." When they were at the foot of the cliff, Naiyenesgani said, "Grandmother, I have killed something, let us go to it." When they came there he said, "Now, grandmother, I will give you some good property. Put down your basket here." He then filled it with feathers. "Now, you may carry it away but do not go along the hillside, go along the top of the hills," he told her. She carried it away along the hillside, and the birds came and took away the feathers. She came back to him and he filled her basket again. "Do not carry the basket on the hillside," he told her. Again, she carried it along the side of the hill and the birds came and took away all the feathers. She came back to him again and he filled the basket for her. "'Do not carry it along the sloping places,' I told you," he said. Then they took the feathers away front her. When she came back to him this time he said, "You do not want to possess this good property which I have been giving you. For that reason your feathers will be poor. You will live in the clefts of the rocks and will use bark for your house. Your garments will be poor. You do not want things that are good. You will not have a shirt."

He went again where there was something bad. When he came among the people there they said to him, "If you have supernatural power, take out our people from the marsh where they have sunk." [1] "Very well," he said, "I will take them out for you." When he came to the place he stood first at the east, then at the south, then at the west, and finally at the north. Then the water disappeared of itself and he went to the entrance and went in. "I have come for the people you have taken away," he said, "bring them to me. Do not bring me just one." "There are no people," replied the monster. "Just bring them to me, do not talk." Then he brought them to him. "Just one sits there," he said. "I did not come for one," he told him. Then he sent one out to him. "Are there many people where you are staying?" he asked. "There are many people there," he said. "Bring them all out," Naiyenesgani called. The people all began to crowd outside. Then they went up to the surface of the ground. "You may just stay in the marsh," he said to the monster. When all the people had come out he spoke to him (the monster), "You must not do it any time. Just soft mud does not talk. It must not speak words." Then he went out away from him and came where the people were.

"Four of you take charge of your people," he said. "Do not go close in among the houses." Then four of them came there. Now pick out your own people and go home with them," he told them. "Now you pick your people," he said to another. Then that one picked out his people. Then he went to another place, "You pick out your people," he told the third." That one selected his relatives. Then he called to another in the same manner and he picked out his folks. Then they were all satisfied.

Naiyenesgani was sitting there. "I just speak to you," he said, "select for me four pretty girls. I wish to go with them." Then he went away with them toward the west. At Kagodjae he left one; at Tsosbai, another; and at Becdelkai, the third. With the other one he went to the west where they remain forever.

[1] Mooney gives this incident with greater detail, (a), p. 204. The one who assisted was Gopher, who made four tunnels one above the other in which Naiyenesgani hid in succession. In Russell's version Lizard plays a part, (a), p. 256. The Navajo call the monster Teelget, Matthews, l. c., p. 117.
[2] Mooney's account is similar, (a), pp. 205-8, as is also that of Russell, (a), pp. 257-8. The Navajo also have this story, Matthews, pp. 119-121.
[3] Mooney has a similar account, (a), p. 20:3. The other Apache and the Navajo seem not to have such a monster.

5. Naiyenesgani Rescues the Taos Indians

Naiyenesgani went among the Pueblo Indians. While there he stole and concealed their corn. When they came to him, they said, "Apache go outside." Naiyenesgani made a motion over the corn with his hand, and it became snakes. Then they were friendly to him. He put his hand over the place again and there were piles of corn as before. Again, they said, "Apache go outside." He made passes before the piles of corn and they turned into snakes which moved about. Again, they became friendly with him. He moved his hand over the place and the corn lay in rows again. "Go outside Apache," they said again. He moved his hand over the corn. The rows changed into snakes having wings. "Shut the door," he said. They commenced throwing the corn away. They shut the door. They came to Naiyenesgani who passed his hands over the place again and the corn lay in rows.

"You certainly are a medicineman," they said. "Over here is a sinking place where our people have been taken into the ground away from us."

"Very well," said Naiyenesgani, and began taking off his clothes. He took off his moccasins, his leggings, his shirt, and his hat, and said to them, "Cover them all with turquoise for me." They put down a few pieces for him. "Cover them entirely," he said, speaking as a chief. Then they covered a little more of his clothing. he spoke again saying, "Cover them completely." Then they completely covered his clothing and gave the turquoise to him. His moccasins, leggings, hat, shirt, and all were completely covered, as he had asked of them.

He then went to the sinking place. He made a black hoop, a blue one, a yellow one, and one of mixed colors. He came to the place where there was much water standing. In this lake there lived a monster which sucked in the Pueblo people. Standing at the east, he made four motions with the black hoop, and then threw it in. The water opened out at the center of the lake. He then stood at the south and making motions four times threw in the blue hoop. The water receded from the center. He stood at the west, made motions four times with the yellow hoop, and threw it in. The water moved still further from the center. Finally, he stood at the north with the hoop of mixed colors. He made motions four times and threw it in. The water came together and vanished.

In the center of the place where the water had stood, the top of a ladder was sticking up. When Naiyenesgani started to go there a crane which was on guard was about to give warning. He gave him a red stone for a present and the crane did not make a noise. When Naiyenesgani came near him, YeLagôLtsôde, the monster, held him by the sole of his foot. He kicked and the monster fell. When he went in, he saw an old man and an old woman lying there, human beings. "I have come to visit you. I do not see any of the people," he said. "I am going to burn you up." Then Naiyenesgani took the firedrill and twirled it until the place was full of smoke. "Now, go out," he said to the captives. From each of four doors two people passed out. "There are no other people," said the monster. "Are these all?" he asked. "There are innumerable people," one replied. "All of you go out," he told the people, and again he. filled the place with smoke. "Hurry go out with it," he told them. More people came out. "Are these all?" he asked again. Those who had come out said, "There are still people there." Then he filled the place with smoke again by means of the firedrill. "Go out with it," he said. "All of you go out." He asked again if there were no more inside. They had all come out. Then he sent the old man and old woman into the water. The Pueblo Indians followed him about. He sent them to their homes and they went off one by one.

6. The Monster Fish

[1]
A monster fish which lived in a lake swallowed anyone coming near it. Naiyenesgani came there and was swallowed by the fish which swain to the center of the lake and lay in deep water. Naiyenesgani, sitting inside of the fish, began singing ceremonial songs, that the fish might move to the shore of the lake. When he had finished his songs, he cut off the heart of the fish which raced with him toward the shore, throwing the smaller fish and water far away. It fell with him at the shore of the lake. Naiyenesgani, with his obsidian knife, cut openings in the neck of the fish through which he went out, carrying the heart in his hand. He gave it to the suit, saying, "Here, carry this where he cannot get it again." That is why a fish has a series of openings on the sides of its neck. He went home to his grandmother, YoLgaiistdzan. The firedrill had blazed up and then died down again. [2]

[1] This exploit of Naiyenesgani seems not to he known to the other Southern Athapascan tribes who consider fish and water animals taboo. Mooney's account tells of a fish leaving the water and flying to secure its prey, (a), p. 200.
[2] This was a sign for the grandmother of the danger or safety of Naiyenesgani. Cf. Matthews, pp. 117, 122.

6. The Monster Fish (Second Version)

[1]
A monster fish which lived in a lake swallowed anyone coming near it. Naiyenesgani came there and was swallowed by the fish which swain to the center of the lake and lay in deep water. Naiyenesgani, sitting inside of the fish, began singing ceremonial songs, that the fish might move to the shore of the lake. When he had finished his songs, he cut off the heart of the fish which raced with him toward the shore, throwing the smaller fish and water far away. It fell with him at the shore of the lake. Naiyenesgani, with his obsidian knife, cut openings in the neck of the fish through which he went out, carrying the heart in his hand. He gave it to the suit, saying, "Here, carry this where he cannot get it again." That is why a fish has a series of openings on the sides of its neck. He went home to his grandmother, YoLgaiistdzan. The firedrill had blazed up and then died down again. [2]

[1] This exploit of -Naiyenesgani seems not to he known to the other Southern Athapascan tribes who consider fish and water animals taboo. Mooney's account tells of a fish leaving the water and flying to secure its prey, (a), p. 200.
[2] This was a sign for the grandmother of the danger or safety of Naiyenesgani. Cf. Matthews, pp. 117, 122.

8. Naiyenesgani Removes Certain Dangers

At that time a trail passed between a cliff and a stream. TsedagediLîsdîhî, a monster, sat by this trail. His home was in the large stream flowing by. When anyone passed along the trail in front of him, he kicked him into the water where the children of the monster ate the victim and only his red bones floated to the surface. The people passed along there and TsedagediLîsdîhî kicked them down.

Then Naiyenesgani came there and asked, "Where does the trail go through?" "There," he told him. He came there and made motions as if to pass through. The monster, kicking, missed him. "Where does the trail pass?" he asked. "There," he told him. He came there and made motions as if to pass. The monster, kicking, missed him. "Where does the trail pass?" he asked. "There," he told him. He made motions as if to pass again. The monster missed when he kicked at him. Then Naiyenesgani kicked him into the water. When his children had finished eating him they said, "It was our father's meat." His bones, very red, floated to the top. Naiyenesgani came there and sent the young ones out. [1]

Then he was about to lie with his wife. He pounded some sumac sticks and twisted them together. Having them in his hand he went with her and when she lay down for him, he inserted the sticks first. Her vulvae were provided with teeth by means of which she killed men. She cut these sticks with her teeth and he destroyed them. After that she had no such teeth. Before that, cutting the men with her teeth, she had killed them. [2]

Then the reeds needed for arrows stood at the junction of two canyons. When anyone came there for arrows the rocks closed on him and killed him. Notwithstanding the danger, people continued coming for arrows and were killed. Naiyenesgani came there, made as if to pass four times, and then went to the reeds and broke some of them off. The rocks did not come together. He carried the reeds out and distributed them so that everybody had arrows. He did that. [3]

[1] Matthews gives a similar incident, not associated with a stream, p. 122. It has been recorded from the San Carlos Apache.
[2] A very widespread conception. See Lowie, (a), p. 237; Dorsey, (c), p. 35.
[3] Usually this danger of approaching rocks is passed on the journey to the sun. Matthews, p. 109.

9. The Killing of the Bear

[1]
When some children were playing one of them said, "I will be a bear." He made a pile of dirt which the other children carried away in their hands until it was all gone. In their absence, he made claws for himself of hide fleshers

and muscles of the larger hide dresser. With these, he dug a deep hole into which he went so far that he could not be seen. When he came out, he was covered with hair to his elbows and knees. He went in again and came out with hair to his shoulders and hips. When he came out the third time, his body was nearly covered, and the fourth time completely covered with hair.

He went among the people, running in and out, and killing the children. He went off to the Navajo country and hid his heart near some oak trees at a place called, "open-mouth-bear". He then came back and again began to kill the people. Although they shot arrows at him, they could not hurt him.

Naiyenesgani went to the Navajo country carrying his war club. The bear, seeing the danger, started to run to the place where his heart lay. Naiyenesgani ran after him and came to the heart first. As he came near it be heard the oak leaves lying over it, making a noise like "ca a ca a". It was the beating of the heart that made them move. Naiyenesgani, making motions four times, struck the heart, and the bear, running close behind, fell dead.

[1] The story given by Russell, (a), p. 262, agrees very well except that Fox (Coyote) is the hero; but the bears referred to by Mooney (a, p. 208) seem not the same in any particular. Matthews has the incident of the gradual transformation of a girl into a bear and that of the detached vitals but not in connection with Naiyenesgani, pp. 99-101. Naiyenesgani does kill the bear that pursues one of the monsters, but the account is abbreviated, p. 124. The same motive with different details appears in Gros Ventre, Kroeber, (a), p. 105.

10. The Traveling Rock

A large number of the people started away, camping. They discovered the enemy who came together in large numbers on the plains and surrounded them. They made a barricade of their goods and commenced to fight. The enemy came straight at them. When they were near, they fought with knives. The women fought too, drawing the bows this way with their feet. Putting the bow over one foot, the woman drew the string with both hands and shot at the enemy. Nearly all were killed. Many of the enemy also were killed. A few of the Jicarilla escaped and returned to their own country. Another generation grew up from these. When they were again numerous, they started away to camp in the plains. Again, the enemy discovered them and came together. They fought with them again until only a small hand was left. Many of the enemy were also killed. Those who escaped came again to their own country. Another generation grew up and there were many men again.

The stone which rolls around came among them and killed many of the people. It went among those who were camping over on the plain and killed many of them. It came among the people who were living on the east side of the. Rio Grande. Naiyenesgani tried to head it off but he could not get around it to shoot. When it was nearly on the people he got in front of it. It passed right through them. Again he got in front of it and once more it came among the people. When he got in front of it this time he shot it, hitting it in the backbone. It still lies over by Picuris with its mouth open. It is a blue stone that has a white stripe across its breast. They cut off this white material which shows on the surface. When one gets sore from wearing the medicine string about his body, he puts some of this on and be gets well. If one gets shot with an arrow he gets well at once by the aid of this. The Picuris and other Pueblo Indians scrape this off and use it for their medicine also.

11. The Origin of Sheep and Cattle

Naiyenesgani went around looking in vain for monsters. When he failed to find any he started off in this direction, toward the Mescalero country. He climbed to the top of White Mountain and looked about in all the different directions in vain. There were no monsters. Then he threw away his staff. "You will get your living by means of this," he said, and right where he threw it, it became a yucca.

Then he washed from his hands the pollution from the killing of the monsters and threw it in different directions. "With this you will live," he said, referring to the Mexicans. That is why sheep and cattle have a bad odor. The dirt he washed from his hands became cattle and sheep. All the monsters were gone. The Mescalero live upon the staff which he threw away, the Mexicans live upon the cattle and the sheep. That is why Mexicans have many sheep and cattle. He spoke to them this way.

12. Naiyenesgani Takes His Leave

Naiyenesgani, when he was about to go away, came here to the center where the heart of the world lies. When he had brought the people together he asked them concerning that by which people should live. Standing there at the center of the world, with his black flint armor blowing out from him in the four directions, he said, "Now try your supernatural power on me." Then the men who knew magic tried their powers but the bad missiles fell all about him. When he blew his breath towards them they fell. "You see you can do nothing with them. People will not live by means of such things as these," he said.

Then he put the bear in charge of all the insects and of all kinds of fruit. He gave marten (?) the care of the yuccas, chokecherries, and corn. He placed one of the small squirrels in control of blackberries, strawberries, and small fruits. Grasshopper was given grain. He assigned the amole to black tail deer. "These are the things by means of which people will live," he said.

"The heart of the world lies here. Wherever you may wander you will come back to this place," he told them. "I am going away now to my grandmother. I have already rid the world of monsters for you. In the future, when the people have become few, I will come back to you that we may all die together. I made this world as it lies here quite strong for you. For that reason you shall live here on this world."

He made this river, the Rio Grande, its backbone. He made a mountain ridge for its neck and Pike's Peak for its head. He made the Sangro de Christo Range one of its legs and the mountains on the west side of the river the other leg. White Flint Mountain is one of its nipples, and Rock Bell Mountain the other. He made the world very strong. [1]

"You shall live right here," he told them. "If they take you away from this place, to another, where the surroundings are not your own, you will perish." [2]

We are dying off because the Americans have taken us to a place not our own and have forced us to live by means not ours. They have taken us away from the world which our father made for us to live in and we are dying in consequence. Some of the Indians who are intelligent do not like it. We are dying every summer. When we were living in our own country the people did not die as they do now.

Having talked to them in this manner he went away to his grandmother. [3]

[1] Naiyenesgani made the world of the body of YoLgaiistdzan his grandmother, and it is probably the chief object of worship among the Jicarilla. This information was suppressed by the informant but supplied later by Edward Ladd who is an excellent authority.

[2] This addition to the myths, of material pertinent to modern conditions, is evidence of the vitality and freedom of religion among the Jicarilla. The same views in nearly the same form were given by two other old men. They hold that there is a definite cause for the evils which have come upon the tribe. They have been removed from that portion of the earth where the sacred rivers and mountains, filled with supernatural power for their help, were situated. There is no remedy, for it is a fate foretold long ago. YoLgaiistdzan and her grandson, while powerless are not unsympathetic; they will return to share the fate of extinction.

[3] The Navajo locate the present home of Estsanatlehi in the western ocean, but Naiyenesgani and his brother live at the mouth of the San Juan, Matthews, pp. 133-134.

13. Naiyenesgani Takes His Leave (Second Version)

Naiyenesgani came to the rock that was rolling over people. It rolled away from him and he could not overtake it to kill it. After trying for some time to pass it, he succeeded in getting ahead of it and shooting it. Before he killed it he said, "What shall I do with you who swallow people?" Killing it, he said, "This is what I do with bad people, I kill them." He did not go up to it nor did he cut it. [1]

"Now I will go and look for other bad things," Naiyenesgani said. "Wait for me, my friend." Then four of them started away toward the east. They climbed one of the sacred mountains and looked around without finding anything. After that, they came to Balgai, another mountain, which they climbed. When they had looked about without finding anything, Naiyenesgani said, "There are no bad things. Now, we will go back. He threw all the yucca stalks back of him, saying, "People will live on you right here." [2] The name of this mountain will be Balgai." Then they started back and taking only four steps, they reached Taos.

"Do you like it?" he asked the people. "I have killed for you all the monsters which were in the world. That is why my name is, 'Monsters-he-kills'. Are you all pleased?" "Yes," they replied. "I made these things which are on the earth so that you may like them. I have made everything that you will eat; the berries, amole fruit, and plums. Are you satisfied? I made all these for you when you were poor and had nothing. Are you pleased with all these fruits I have made for you." "They are very good, my grandson," she said. "You will eat them every summer. I do not wish that you shall live on these things all the time because I am not going to talk about them for you always."

[1] Mooney, (a), p. 208. Matthews has an incident differing in several particulars, p. 125.
[2] This refers to the food of the Mescalero as explained in the preceding myth.

14. The Winning of Daylight

[1]

Long ago they all gathered to play the moccasin game. [2] When they arranged the wagers, daylight was staked against darkness as a perpetual future condition. Day was about to break. Roadrunner with his red spot did not miss the moccasin once. Crane also guessed right every time. Roadrunner and Crane both rubbed their cheeks with fire.

Owl took the ball from the moccasin. "It will not be day," he sang, "who, wo." Roadrunner took the ball again. "Daylight is good," he sang, "the east is whitening." While they were intent on the game, day broke and they started to run to the mountains. All those who were struck by the sun's rays became red. Roadrunner had rubbed his cheeks with fire and that is why they are so red. Crane also burned his cheeks by rubbing them with fire and they are red in consequence. Those were beaten who sang, "There will be no daylight." That is why they go around at night. Those that go around in the daytime won.

[1] According to Mooney's account this event took place in the lower world before the emergence, (a), p. 198. This myth is known to the Navajo (Franciscan Fathers, p. 485) and to the other Apache.

[2] A game in which the players form two parties one of which hides a ball in one of the moccasins standing in a row and the other guesses which moccasin contains it.

15. Coyote Secures Fire

[1]

Fireflies had their camp where high rocks stood around it in a circle and there was no trail leading down to it. They were the only people who had fire. They were playing the hoop and pole game with Otters. In vain Coyote walked around the rocks seeking a place to go down. He went where some children were playing beyond a hill and asked them where the trail was that lead down. They would not tell him. Having gathered some red berries and having made two strings of beads from them, he came again to the children. "Now tell me where the trail is," he said as he gave them the beads. "Right by the edge of the rocks stands a cedar tree," they told him, "one takes hold of it and it bends with him to the ground. If one says to it, 'Bend down to me' it will bend down and you may go out with it." Coyote pulled off some cedar bark and made a bundle of it to serve as a torch.

He went over where they were playing the hoop and pole game. They were betting their hides and when one was beaten his hide was pulled off and he jumped into the river and came out again dressed as he was before. Coyote wanted to bet his hide. "No," the other players told him, "your skin sticks too tightly to your nose, you might cry badly about it." He played, however, and lost, and when they were stripping off his skin it stuck to his nose and he cried. He jumped into the river but came out as he went in, red and without a skin. Then the others caught him and pushed him into a badger's hole. He came out with a coat of short fur. He wished to bet again but the others would not permit him saying, "You cry so about it that every one is ashamed." [2]

When it was nearly night Fireflies built a fire in the center of their camp preparatory to a dance. When the people were all standing about after the dance began, Coyote tied the cedar bark he had prepared to his tail, and dancing about, tried to get his tail in the fire. "Coyote, your tail is on fire," they called to him. "I am working magic with it; it will not burn," he replied. His tail blazed up, and he jumped over the heads of the spectators and ran to the place where the trail led up. Fireflies ran after him. "Come bend down to me," he called to the cedar. When it came down to him he went up, tossing up his tail as he topped the rock. He ran off, throwing his tail from side to side. Those running after him tried to put the fire out. Coyote ran on, whipping the trees with his tail, still pursued, until he came to the border of the sky. When he had run almost entirely around the world with the fire he was tired and crawled into a hole.

The whole world was afire and burning. It was burned black everywhere. That is why you can make a fire with a drill from all kinds of trees. Here at the east some trees were left unburned. They are like stone and will not burn if they are put in the fire. Petrified wood was the only thing of all that was on the world that was not burned.

[1] Russell obtained this story with additional details. The hero in his account should be Coyote instead of Fox, an error probably due to the interpreter. The birds with whom he was flying, if named tetl, (deL) were cranes instead of geese, (a). p. 261. While this form of the story seems to be peculiar to the Southwest, a similar origin for fire is found in many other localities. Teit, (a), pp. 56-57; Goddard, p. 195; Lowie, (a), p. 244; Kroeber, (c), pp. 252-260.

[2] Matthews has this incident in another connection, p. 97.

16. Coyote Secures Fire. (Second Version.)

Coyote came where there were three children. "Show me where the trail goes up," he said. "I will give you these beads if you will show me the trail." Then he gave them the beads. They showed him a piñon tree by means of which the people went up and down. He went down by the aid of the piñon tree by means of which the people went up and down. He looked for some white clay with which, when he found it, he whitened his face, making zigzag lines.

He came where they were dancing and mingled with them. "Coyote, your tail is burning," one of them said to him. "I have supernatural power for that. It won't burn," he replied. He went among them again, poking the fire with his tail until it took fire, when he jumped over them and ran away with it. "Coyote does not know the trail up the wall," they said. He ran away with the fire and they all ran after him.

When Coyote was tired out, he gave the fire to Duck who ran with it. When Duck was tired he gave it to Dove. Dove ran with it until he was tired and gave it to Kingfisher who ran with it. "Fire came from me," he said. Kingfisher flew entirely around the border of the sky with the fire.

"Fire came from me. All the people secured their fire from me." The people ate with it and their food became sweet. The people all over the world were pleased. Something good happened.

17. The Swallowing Monster

At another time the people were camping near a spring, hunting deer. When one of the girls went to the spring for water she found a dead deer lying there. She ran back and told the others what she had found and some one went out and brought in the deer. This happened four times; the girl found a dead deer as she was going for water and it was brought in and eaten. [1]

After dark someone looked out through a hole in the tipi and saw the monster. They built a big fire on that account for it was very dark. They told the fire poker, "You must cry like a little baby." "You," they told the pole over which hides are dressed, "must shout like a boy." "You must laugh like a girl," they told the muller. "When he runs after its, you must shout like a grown person," they told the pestle.

While it was still very dark they ran off. The monster, after hunting for them in vain at the camp site, ran after them. The fire poker cried like a baby and the monster ran back. The crying ceased and he ran after them again. He heard a boy shouting at the old camp and returned. Not finding anyone, be ran after them again. Back at the camp a girl was laughing. Having looked for her in vain he ran after them again. A man was shouting at the old camp. The monster ran back and searched for him in vain. He then swallowed the fire poker, the tanning pole, the muller, and the pestle. He ran after them again but by this time the, v were far away. He overtook them and swallowed all of them but the little girl. She came to Spider, who was chopping a tree near his home, and he hid her under the knot of his hair braid. When the monster came there be said, "Where did you put the girl?" "I did not see anyone, "he replied. "Her tracks are here," the monster replied. "Nobody came to me," old man Spider said. "I am going to swallow you," Said the monster. Then Spider was angry. He tore the monster to pieces and took the girl home with him. [2]

Spider's wife was jealous of the girl. A tree stood by the shore of a lake. Spider's wife made a swing by fastening a poor rope to a limb of the tree. She induced the girl to swing on it. When she swung the second time the rope broke and she fell into the water and became a frog. [3]

[1] It was explained that the deer were left there that the people might get fat and be in good condition for eating.
[2] The Kiowa-Apache tell that Thunder killed the monster with a thunderbolt which explains the manner of killing mentioned here.
[3] This swing incident is found among the Assiniboine, Lowie, (c), p. 157.

18. The Man Who Helped the Eagles

[1]
An Apache was very poor and went about among the Pueblo Indians picking up the food they threw away. That was all he had to eat.

Over by the river there was an eagle nest on top of a sheer cliff. The Pueblo Indians treated the Apache well giving him plenty of food. He went with them to the eagle's nest. They tied a rope to him and lowered him down where the two little eagles were sitting. He took off the rope and stayed there with the eagles. Those above pulled up the rope just by itself. In vain, they let down the rope to him. He remained with the eagles. The others left him and went away. They came back again and let down the rope in vain. Again they left him.

He was very thirsty. He heard someone laugh here below. He jumped up to him. The person said to him, "You have been taking care of the children. Drink this," and gave him a piece of ice about so large (forefinger). "This will not be enough to satisfy me," he thought. He drank it and was satisfied. He lay down beside the little eagles.

The father of the eagles came home. "DagônadeL, you are staying with my children. I thank you," he said. Then he opened the house and they went in. (His house was behind the solid rock.) He gave him some food in a very small clay dish. "That is not enough for me," he thought. The man took off his coat and hung it on the wall. Then he was like any other man. He gave his coat to the man. "Run around with my children for me," he said. He flew across to a stone standing on the other side and back again. He flew way off and came back. He was strong.

The man who lived there called and from the center of the sky a large number of them came down. Some of them wished to carry him on their interwoven wings while some of them wished him to fly and others did not want him to. They put wings on him that were stretched out long and started out with him, up into the sky. The eagles flew under him carrying him up. When he was near the sky hole he began to fall he was so tired. The others got under him carrying him up. Then Panther let down his tail through the sky hole. The man seized it and he was pulled up. Panther had his home there.

They had enemies there with whom they fought. The hornets were their enemies. Some of them were black, some of them were yellow. The yellow ones had yellow houses, the black ones had black houses. Panther had much buckskin from which he made him shirts of many thicknesses. There were holes just for the eyes. The man went with the eagles to find the enemy. They camped close by them. He was carrying a quirt in his hand. Early the next morning when they went after wood they met the enemy and began to fight with them. The hornets were killing them. The man put on the shirt Panther had made for him and began whipping around with the quirt. He strung the bodies of those he had killed on a stick. He had two sticks of them. The eagles came back to their home. One of them said, "DagônadeL was killed first of all." Panther said, "My grandchild is very brave. Watch for the men he has killed." When he came back there from fighting the enemy, they commenced dancing around in a circle. Meadowlark danced around sunwise. "You had better go down, you say bad words against the people," they told him.

[1] Under the title, The Great Shell of Kintyel, Matthews gives this story in a different locality and with additional details. It is the myth explaining the

origin of the Bead Chant, pp. 195-208. The San Carlos have a ceremony for babies of which this is the myth. According to Edward Ladd, this man was Naiyenesgani.

19. The Bear-Man

They were living on the other side of the Rio Grande near a mountain called Nabîanye where they were raising a crop. A bear was killing them one by one. There at a place called Teîcnadjin, "trees thick," the bear had his camp from which he came to get the people. They went there after cherries. One of them, the tallest, climbed a tree to get the cherries. The bear killed them.

They ran back away from him. They sent word to the camp and all got ready to go after him. They followed his tracks. Here a bear had run along. Over there, they found his coat (bearskin) which he wore when he came after the people. He took off also the braided sticks which he wore under his coat, as he ran to his home. They tracked him to his camp which was by an arroyo. He had made a number of holes, in a row on the opposite bank. Those pursuing him came there in the early morning and stood by his door.

An old man found him. "He is like one of our people, but we will kill him for an enemy," he said. [1] They brought him to the door and shot him. He had killed a bear and taken its coat. He had cut small tough sticks and fixed them under his coat so the arrows would not go through. They brought it home.

[1] By "our people" is meant that he spoke a related language, probably Kiowa-Apache or Mescalero.

20. Releasing the Buffalo

[1]

Long ago, they were camping about over on the plain without food. They were playing the hoop and pole game. Raven came from nobody knew where and took off his quiver. Inside of the quiver were intestines. Magpie took them out. They watched Raven to see which way he would start home. When it was evening he started off flying up toward the sky-hole. "You must all watch him," they said to each other. Everyone was looking at him. He kept circling about until he became very small and few could see him. When he was so far off that no one else could see him, Rattlesnake and Bat still could make him out. When he was at the top of the sky and out of sight, he flew across this way to the east where. the Black Mountains range from north to south. When he reached them he went to the junction of canyons. Only the two could see him.

The people moved their camp four times before they came to him. They found he had very much meat there which he (Raven) distributed to the people. They asked him about the buffalo but he would not tell them. Then they changed an Apache into a puppy, making eyes for him of black obsidian. They hid him under a brush bed and moved their camp away.

The children of Raven came around the deserted camp and finding the dog, took him up. Raven's smallest child folded his arms about him and carried him home. His father said to the children, "He was lying there to find out something." The child did not want to give up the dog. The father put the poker in the fire and when it was burning brought it near the dog's eyes. After a while he cried, Wau." "You may keep it, its only a dog. It does not know anything," the father said. "It's name will be înôldî (choke)," said the child.

Raven had the buffalo all shut up. He opened the door when he wanted to kill some of them. That was the way he secured the meat. The dog went along with them and they fed it. When it was dark and they had all gone to bed, the dog went over there and opened the door. The buffalo started out. They had nearly all gone out before Raven noticed it. He ran over there with his quiver, shooting at them as they rail past. When all his arrows were gone but one, he looked at the door for the man who had become a dog. There was an old buffalo going out which could hardly get to its feet. The man caught hold of this buffalo and went out with it clinging to the opposite side. Raven paid no attention to it and stood there holding his bow with the one arrow looking for the man in vain.

The man overtook the others who had moved their camp away, "I turned the buffalo all loose," he told them. They turned back, moving their camp to the buffalo, where they killed many of them and were no longer hungry.

Raven told his children, "You will live on the meat that is left on the backbone and on the eyeballs."

Long ago they were hungry but he let the buffalo out and then they had plenty to eat. That way he did.

[1] In the version obtained by Russell, (a), p. 259, many other animals are released. This story seems not to be known to the Western Apache and the Navajo. The Mescalero say that Coyote failed and Naiyenesgani succeeded in inducing the buffalo to leave the lower world.

The Blackfoot have a somewhat different version of this myth. Wissler and Duvall, pp. 50-53. The Gros Ventre do not appear to connect Raven with the retention of the buffalo, an old woman and her daughter being mentioned. Kroeber, (a), p. 65.

21. Releasing the Buffalo. (Second Version.)

Raven had the buffalo hidden they say. Then the people found out about it and went to his house. The house and Raven's children were covered with ashes and grey and dirty. The smallest child took the stone away from the opening to the lower world. Then the buffalo were in a large herd on the plain.

"The eyeballs and the fat between the shoulders will be mine," Raven said. "You did me a wrong. I lived on the buffalo. You took away the stone and now you have caused me to be without anything to eat. You have made me poor. I go about starving. That is why I eat whatever anybody kills," Raven said this they say.

22. The Origin of Corn and Deer

[1]

Once there was a man who went around with a little turkey. The man lost all he had in gambling. His people brought together more things for him and again he gambled them all away. Then they agreed they would kill him if he lost again. They tied some things to his tipi poles for him. He came back and looked at them. "Now I will play the hoop and pole game again," he said. His turkey went around in front of him and said, "My father, why is it that you have such a poor mind? If you lose all this again, they are going to kill you."

He started away and came to the side of a river. A pretty tree was standing there. He commenced to chop it with a stone ax. At sunset, only a little part of it remained to be chopped. He went home and came again in the morning. The tree stood as it had when he first saw it. He commenced chopping at it again. At sunset there was only a little more to be chopped. He went home. He came back the next morning and commenced chopping. When only a little more remained to be chopped it was night and he went home. He came back the next day and the tree stood as if it had never been cut.

Right by the tree there was a cliff. TcactcîyaLkîdn, the talking god, stood there and spoke to him, "My friend," he said, "why are you always bothering my tree?" "I have use for this, my friend," the other replied, "that is why I bother it." "What will you do with it?" asked the god. am going down the river by means of it," he said. The god made motions four times and felled it. He cut off a length just long enough for a man to lie in. He put back the remainder of the tree on the stump and it came together again as if it had never been cut.

"My friend, get all the birds that peck trees to hollow it out for you." Then all the birds came together and pecked at the inside of it, going through the tree. The man tried to get inside but it was not yet big enough. The birds went through it four times again in each direction. The hole was now large enough to receive his body. Then he distributed the beads among the birds that had worked for him.

Then the god came again to help him. He used the foam on the water to smooth the log. Spider closed both ends of the log for him. "It's ready, my child," said the god. "There are four bad places in succession," he told him.

30

Making motions four times the god put the log with the man inside of it into the water. It floated down stream with him. It came down to the place where the whirlpool is and the log began to spin around. It went on down stream from there with him until it came to the waterfall where it stuck. The god got it loose for him and it floated down to a place where the Pueblo Indians were pulling out driftwood. They pulled the log out but the god put it back. It went on down until it came where there was much driftwood floating. It floated down with him from there. When it landed he tried in vain to get out. After a while, he succeeded.

As he walked along beside the river he began to wish he had something to plant. He caught a lot of ducks, and pulled out their feathers which he used for a bed. He ate the birds but saved the sinew from their legs and used it for making arrows. When he had been there four days and the sun was setting he saw his turkey silhouetted against the sky. He came toward him. They walked together along the river. As they walked along he said he wished he had seeds to plant.

"My father," said the turkey, "clear a piece of ground." He cleared it. Then the turkey stood with his wings outstretched, facing in each direction. When he walked from the east, black corn lay in a row; he walked from the south, blue corn lay in a row; he walked from the west, yellow corn lay in a row; he walked from the north, and corn of different colors lay in a row. "Now plant this," he said.

He planted all the different kinds of corn. When it had been planted one day, it commenced to come up. After the second day, the corn had two leaves. On the third day, it was quite high. On the fourth day, it had brown tassels. The turkey went around gobbling.

The man lay down in the feathers and slept. On the other side, to the east, stood a rocky ridge. He saw a fire over there. In the morning he went where the fire had been but there was no fire nor any tracks. That evening there was a fire there again. He stood up a forked stick and placed himself sitting on his heels so that the fire appeared In a line with the fork of the stick. The next day, getting his bearings in this way, he went again to the place where he had seen the fire. There were no tracks there. He went home again. When the sun went down he sat in the same place and saw the fire again. The next morning he went where the fire had been. There were no tracks there. He went back home.

The corn and the tobacco were now ripe. He rolled a cigarette and tied it to his belt. The third day, at sunset, there was a fire there again. When he went to the place a girl was sitting where the stream flowed out from the mountains. She was rubbing a deerskin. The man stood by her but she could not see him. The cicada had loaned him its flute. He stood there and blew upon it. As the girl was working at the buckskin she pushed her hand down and turned her head to listen. She looked under the grass but could not find the cicada. She sat down again and began to rub the buckskin. The man blew again upon the flute. Again, she looked for it without finding it. He stood on this side of her and blew on the flute again. She got up and started toward her home. He followed behind her and then she saw him. Causing the solid rock to open she went in. He went in behind her but left his arrows lying by the door. When he got inside a very old woman who was sitting there jumped up and ran out. (She was afraid of her son-in-law).

Then the old man came home. He immediately took up his tobacco and filled his pipe. When he was ready he blew some smoke and said to the young man, "Will you smoke with me?" "No," he said. "Where do you come from, I have looked everywhere in this country. Where have people come into existence?" He took up another sack of tobacco and filled another pipe. He smoked and blew the smoke. "Do you want to smoke?" he asked. "No," replied the man. Then he took up another pipe and another sack of tobacco, filled the pipe again, and blew smoke. "Do you want to smoke?" he asked. "No," he answered.

Then the man began to smoke the cigarette he had tied to his belt. The old man smelled the smoke and said, "I wish it was my turn to smoke." He gave him the cigarette and the old man inhaled the smoke. His legs straightened cut. The voting man blew smoke against the soles of his feet and the palms of his hands. He commenced to get up. "That was something good," he was saving as he stood up. "I wish you would bring me much of it from the place where you got it." "That is all there is,," the young man said.

They placed a dish of food before him and he swallowed it at one mouthful. He took up his arrows and started home. Outside, only one footprint was to be seen. [2] He came where his turkey was. Then they tracked him to the place where the corn was growing. When he came to the turkey, it was afraid of him. When it was evening he made two cigarettes and tied them to his clothes. He went again where the others were living. He gave the old man the cigarettes to smoke again and then went home the next morning. This time, there were two tracks outside. "I do not think, he is a human being," the old man said. The next evening he went there again. He carried with him a cigarette which he had made. When the old man had smoked it, he said, "That is good." He went into the tipi.

The turkey was going around a little way off, he was afraid of him. That evening the man went back again carrying four cigarettes. The old man smoked them, saying they were good. The next morning the woman went back with him. They both walked across the river on top of the water. They gathered much corn and tobacco. The woman started home. When she came to the river, she took off her moccasins and waded through. She brought the corn to her people. "It is good," he said, "to eat with deer meat." He gave his father-in-law the corn. The father-in-law, in return, gave him the deer which he possessed. [3]

The old man's name was DînîdeyînîLt'anne, "Game he raised". The other man who came to him was named AtdiLdeyeseLdlî, "He floated down". Then the deer all ran out. The man and woman moved their camp away. The woman made a brush house but the deer came and ate off all the leaves. She made another brush shelter. The deer ate it again. The woman took up the fire poker and hitting the deer with it, said, "Deer will have a sense of smell." Then they went off a little way from her. The next day they went farther away where they could not be seen.

"Turkeys shall live in the mountains and people will live upon them," she said. Then the woman was hungry and she went to the east saving "What has become of my children, all having the same kind of horns?" Then she went to the south and shouted, "Where have you gone, you that have bodies alike? Come back here." Then she went west. "My children, where have you gone, you that have tails alike, come back here." Then she went to the north, "My children, where have you gone, you that have ears alike, come back here."

From that direction, from the north, they came running back. They ran and surrounded her. From the west also they came and surrounded her. She killed a large number of them. "Now you may go and live in the mountains. People will live upon you. You shall have a sense of smell. People will live upon you." Then the corn was all that belonged to them.

[1] Russell secured the first part of this myth in much the form given here, (a), p. 268. The Navajo myth as given by Matthews (Natinesthani, pp. 160-194), is full of details and ii accompanied by songs. It is evidently the myth of an important ceremony.
[2] He traveled with the lightning was the explanation given of this.
[3] It was explained that the young man was striving to get the advantage of the old man in the matter of smoking and of the young woman in resisting desire. On the fourth night the girl made the first advance. The young man having won these points, the old man placed the corn beside the meat and pronounced one as good as the other.

23. The Origin of Corn and Deer (Second Version)

They tell of a man who went about accompanied by a small turkey. The two went down the Rio Grande. There were four bad places for them to pass. When they had gone down the stream, they sat by the bank.

Then the man said to the turkey, "My child, this is a nice land we have come to. There should be some seeds." "Father, I will soon make some corn for you. To-morrow you must level a place." Then the man levelled a piece of ground. The turkey came to the prepared place. He ran from the east toward it. He made black corn lie there in a row. He ran from the south causing blue corn to lie in a row. He ran again from the west making a row of yellow corn. Then he ran from the north and made a row of corn of various colors. "Now, my father, you may plant it," he said. The man planted it, scattering the seed. He raised corn and tobacco also.

He went across the river. He saw the blazing of a fire. "Where are there any people living?" he said to himself. The next day he went where he had seen the fire but there were no people there. When it was dark again, there was a fire blazing again in the same place. When he went there the next day there were no people. He went back to his home and when it was dark again there was a fire as before. The next day he went there and found a woman rubbing hides in the water. She started to run away from him but he ran right after her. She ran into the tipi and he followed after her. Her father spoke to him, offering him tobacco from his fawn-skin tobacco bag. He did not care to smoke and only drew on the pipe once.

He went back to his little home. His turkey was afraid of him and would not come near him. "You smell, my father. You do not smell as you used to," the turkey said. [1] The man broke off four ears of corn and gave them to the girl's father. He liked them very much. He passed his tobacco bag to him. He drew on the pipe but once.

He went back to his home. His turkey would not come near him. "You smell bad," he said. The next day he went to visit them again, carrying much corn with him. The people were glad because he brought so much corn. Then the girl placed before him loin meat and deer meat side by side. The young man ate the meat. He took some of the tobacco he had raised, rolled a cigarette with corn leaves, and gave it to the old man. "This is good," said the girl's father as he smoked it. "Why did he not bring a large quantity of it? When he comes again he must bring plenty." [2] It was the girl's father who said this. The next day he came to them again bringing a fawn-skin bag full of tobacco. "He has done very well," said the father as he received it.

The woman went home with the man and returned bringing much corn with her. The young man then became her husband. They were satisfied. "We, too, have some property," said the father-in-law, "Go and hunt with him." His brother-in-law placed him by a black screen or blind. Something ran toward him and passed. It was a fox. Then he placed him by a blue blind and a wolf rain by him. "Do not shoot it," his monitor told him. [3] Then he sat by a yellow blind and a large panther ran by him. Finally, he placed him by a variegated blind. "Now, make motions four times when it runs towards you." Then he made motions four times, and shot it. "It ran off that way," he said. It fell with its head backward. When he came to it he turned its head toward the sun and then he butchered it. He killed it for his brother-in-law to whom he gave the hide. His brother-in-law's wife carried it home. [4]

Then the old man, his father-in-law, felt happy. "Now come with me and look at my property," he said. They two went in together where the tame deer were kept. There were very many fawns there which he had raised. He gave all these to his son-in-law, saying, "Now these deer are all your property, take charge of them. All the people living upon the earth will live upon deer." The man and his wife went away and commenced living on a hill. The woman built a fire there. All the deer gathered about her and by the next morning had eaten all the leaves from the brush shelter. The woman did not like it and drove them away. They came back to her, however. This continued for four days. The woman, not liking it, took up the poker and struck the deer with it. They had scattered the ashes all about. She drove them far away saying, "I am tired of you." They came back to her nevertheless. Then she was angry and hit them above the nose with the poker. "Deer will always have a sense of smell," she said. She drove them far away but they came back to her. "My mother, do not hit me, we belong to you. To what other one can we go?" one of them said to her. "I like you my children," she said. Then two fawns came back to her. "The time is at hand when I shall turn you loose," she said. Nevertheless, four came back to her. "Four times, you have destroyed my fence for me. That is why I am going to send you away she said. "Now, my children, I send you off." The next day four of them came back to her again. "To-day, I am turning you loose. Go as far as you wish toward the South. I have made you red in the summertime, blue in the fall, black in the middle of the winter, and brown in the spring. I have made your hoofs and the ends of your noses black. I have made your horns, your ears, your face, your teeth, your gait, your tails, your white hips, all very pretty for you. I have made your eyes of coals, for you to see with. Now, all I have given you looks very well." [5]

[1] The man was unclean, ceremonially at least, from his contact with the girl.
[2] In the third person because men relations-in-law are not directly addressed.
[3] It was explained that a bug or fly on the man's head told him what to do. This is a common source of information in Southwestern myths.
[4] The deer was placed on piñon, pine, oak and mixed bunches of limbs for butchering. The person for whom the hunting is done receives the hide and half the meat.
[5] This myth is the foundation of the deer-hunting ceremony. The substance of it, embodied in songs, is sung before a hunt.

24. The Supernatural Person in The Lake

[1]
Long ago, an old woman gave her boy a present that he might become a medicine man. [2] They were camping through the plains with nothing to eat, but roots and wild seeds. They were all hungry. The woman came to her son and said, "My boy, I am hungry. Have not you anything?" Go home, and to-morrow you will have plenty to eat," her boy replied.

The next day her son began to make a corral close by the river. He gathered the men together and told them to drive in the antelope. They drove them in and killed them. After butchering, they carried the meat home with them. The next day he gathered the people again. They drove antelope into the corral and killed great numbers of them. They brought home the meat with them. The next day he gathered the men again. They drove in antelope and killed very many. They carried the meat home. The antelope ran in by themselves. If they whistled, they came running in as far as one could see. They killed a great many and carried home much meat which lay in a great pile. That evening, the old woman came to her boy and said, "That is enough, my wrists ache." Then the boy quit. They cut the meat into slices to dry and tanned the hides.

The old woman came to her son and asked that he return her gift. "I have already given it to the supernatural one," he told her. Then she cursed him. He left her and came to his own country. He came to a place called "sticks swim around". There are tent poles sticking out of the water there. He lives on the bottom of the lake. The people all came after him but when they came back to their own country they could not find him. Then they commenced to follow his tracks. They saw where the tipi poles had been dragged into the water. They looked all around but could not find him.

Two years after, a large band of them went out on the plains to war. They traveled all night and all the next day. When it was evening they built a fire and smoked the pipe. They heard someone talking to them. "You must be my own people," the voice said. "Yes, we are your own people," they replied. Then he dropped nearby them a big buffalo with its head just turned back and tied. "I started to carry this, but my breath gave out. For that reason, my people, make smoke for me. I will smoke with you," he said. Then they filled the pipe for him and smoked with him. "Where are you going?" he asked. "Here, after the enemy that we may bring back horses," they replied. "Their camp is very close, but they are not aware of your approach," he said, "you can go to them in the day time. About noon, you will surround the horses. I want you to bring me the horse that is all black without a white spot." Then he gave them a fore quarter of the buffalo he was carrying and they commenced to eat it. "If at any time you are in need, make a smoke for me. My home is at TcîcnaLeLîe, by Sheep Horn Mountain. If you want anything at any time, blow smoke towards that place." The next day, in broad daylight, they came to the enemy, and about noon, they found the horses and surrounded them. When they started to drive them away they saw the black one with no white spots for which the supernatural one had asked. When they drove the horses this one kept along with the others. When they came by his home they stopped the horses and the black one ran immediately to the lake. They came back to their own country with the remainder of the band.

[1] This lake, probably situated somewhere at the western edge of the plains, was a regular place of offering. The Jicarilla used to throw beads and other property into this lake as they passed it on their way to the buffalo hunting grounds.
[2] When the services of a medicineman are required, eagle feathers and turquoise are placed on his right foot. If he takes them up he accepts the engagement.

25. The Man Who Traveled with The Buffalo

[1]

At another time, they were on a war expedition going toward the enemy's country. It was very hot and they had now gone a long way without finding the enemy. They turned back, dying from thirst. There was only one who had not died and he was weak from thirst. When it was dark he lay down where a clump of trees was standing.

Ravens were living in the trees under which he lay. Near morning, he woke up and heard the ravens talking. "This is the man who killed the buffalo. They have been killing a great many of them over there." Up above him, he heard the ravens naming the men one by one. "This man, he killed one, over there," they were saying. "Another man killed one here. This man killed a very fat buffalo. This man also killed a very fat buffalo." When morning came, the ravens had mentioned the killing of very many. The man was very thirsty.

About noon he came to a prairie dog village where he lay down. A prairie dog came up out of his hole and brought him a small dish of water. He drank that and again started on his journey.

After a time, he saw a buffalo calf standing. The man traveled along with the buffalo calf. They came where the red mountain ridge stands up horizontally. The buffalo was then about so large (four feet high). When they came to the red place, the buffalo was fully grown. There was a plain there and very many buffalo among which the two went. At evening the ground was white with their tipis. The man lay down in the doorway and spent the night. The next morning the buffalo all went off away from him. There were no tents, only signs that buffalo had been lying there. The buffalo went off toward the east, and the man followed after them. That evening, he came to their camp again. He lay down again in a tipi by the door. The next morning instead of their camp there were only signs of buffalo having lain there. They went off again and the man followed them. At evening he came again to their camp and lay down for the night in the doorway. The next day he followed after them again and came to their camp at evening.

When it was dark, a buffalo who was chief, said, "You have married a very brave man's wife." It was a white buffalo who spoke thus as a chief. He had said, "If any man is braver than I, he may marry my wife." Then the chief came to his house and said, "Make arrows and feather them with the tail feathers of the falcon. Make some also and feather them with mixed feathers. Make a bow of locust (?), one of mulberry wood and another of cedar." Then he made arrows and feathered them. "Make a bow also," he told him.

Then the chiefs all gathered at one place. The man and the largest buffalo stood facing each other. "Do not be afraid," he said, "shoot with these arrows." He commenced shooting and continued until he had used up those he made first. Then he began to shoot with the other kind and used them all. He gave them all to him.

Then he said to him, "The Pecos River will be your chief; the Canadian River will be your chief; the Rio Grande will be your chief; the Chama River will be your chief." [2]

[1] A story probably connected with this has been published by Dr. R. H. Lowie. The fight with the Buffalo chief which is so obscure here is entirely pertinent in the Assiniboine narrative, (c), p, 130. The narrator omitted the latter portion of this myth, which is the basis of the ceremony for infants because he did not wish to impart such information. The man succeeded in killing the white buffalo. The infants when four days old are placed on a buffalo blanket during the ceremony which introduces them to the world and its powers. See p. 269.
[2] These are the sacred rivers of the Jicarilla. The Canadian and Rio Grande are male, "men," the Pecos and Chama are female and are so pictured in the ceremonial dry paintings.

Tales

26. Coyote Steals A Man's Wife

[1]
While a company was on a journey, a rock, on which a man happened to be, was raised to the sky. Coyote took the man's wife and moved away with her. The other people also moved away leaving the man on top of the rock where he lived alone. After a long time, he succeeded in getting down and started to follow the trail of those with whom he had camped. When he came to a place where the campfire had been he said to the fire poker, "How long ago did they leave?" "Long, long ago, they went away," it said. When he came again to a place where they had camped, he asked the pestle, "How long ago did they move from here?" "They moved away long, long ago," it said. He went on again until he came to the signs of another camp. "How long ago did they move away?" he asked the muller. "Not very long ago," it replied. He came where they had camped again and asked the stick on which hides are placed for dressing how long ago the people had moved. "They moved away just now," it replied. He went on and soon came to the tipi.

When he came there he found his wife, Coyote being away hunting. When Coyote came back bringing a deer the man said, "Get some small stones and put them in the fire." When the stones were hot he directed that some fat be heated also. When everything was ready, he took a stone out of the fire, wrapped it in fat, and said to Coyote, "Swallow it." Coyote swallowed it. Then he took another stone from the fire, put it in the fat and said to Coyote, "Swallow this too." He swallowed it. He prepared a third stone in the same manner and Coyote swallowed that. When Coyote had swallowed the fourth one, he said, "I thought you were doing something to me." When he had sat there for some time, he said, "Waw," and started to run. He fell dead while he was running.

"Take a bath," he told his wife. When she had bathed and came back to him they moved their camp toward the east.

[1] The San Carlos Apache have this story, Panther being the one whose wife is stolen and who afterward takes revenge. The Jicarilla informant insisted that it was not Panther but an ordinary Apache who played this part.

27. Coyote Takes Arrows from Owl

Owl was the one who had arrows. He had a club also with which he killed men whom he ate. "Up at the low gap I am watching for men, wû hwû wô," he sang. Coyote came walking along in front of him. "Wû hwû wô," sang Owl, "I am looking for men in the low gap." The two came face to face there. "Now," said Owl, "the one who vomits human flesh will kill men." "Very well," said Coyote, "shut your eyes." Owl Shut his eyes. When he vomitted, Coyote put his hand under and took the meat. The grasshoppers which Coyote vomitted he put in Owl's hand.

"Now open your eyes," said Coyote. Owl looked and saw the grasshoppers lying in his hand. Coyote showed him the meat. "What did I tell you," said Coyote, "this is the meat I threw up." "Where did I drink in the grasshoppers?" said Owl.

Coyote ran all around Owl. "Because I run fast like this I eat people," said Coyote. "These legs of yours are too large, I will fix them for you. Shut your eyes." Coyote cut Owl's leg, trimming away the meat. "Dô xa?a?a you must say," Coyote told him. He broke his leg with a stone and took the arrows away leaving him only the club.

Coyote ran around Owl who threw his club at him. He would say, "Come back, my club," and it would come back to him. He threw it again. "Come here my club," he called. He hit him with it. Coyote said, "Wherever a stick falls when one throws it there it will lie." The club did not return to Owl.

"Now you will live right here in the canyon where many arrows will be in front of you. Somebody might kill you," Coyote told him. Owl hitched himself along into the canyon. "Arrows painted black may kill you," said Coyote. Coyote went around in front of him and shot him with his own (Owl's) arrows.

After that everybody was afraid of Coyote who went around killing off the people.

28. Antelopes Take Arrows from Coyote

They got two little antelopes for him and placed them in his way. He came where they were lying. "Now we will have a footrace, my little nephews," Coyote said. Coyote put a panther skin quiver on one of them, a black bow on the other. The antelopes fell down. "You do not run very fast, my nephews," said Coyote, "stand here in front of me." The antelopes ran off in another direction. They were running side by side. Then they turned and ran back side by side. Coyote ran after them. When he was close to them they ran in different directions. Coyote ran after one of them. The one that was running this way fell. Coyote looked at it and then ran toward the place where it fell. It ran away from him again. Coyote was pretty close when he looked at the other one and saw it fall. He ran to the second one which fell. They were getting a long ways apart and Coyote was tired out, running first one way and then the other. The antelopes took the arrows away and went among their friends.

Coyote speaking as a chief said, "I want you to go after the antelope." They all stood in a circle. "I want you to run after the one which carries the quiver," Coyote said. The antelopes stood facing outward. They broke through the circle. They came together again. "All of you look for the antelopes," Coyote said. They surrounded them. "Go after the one which has the quiver," he said. The antelopes were facing outward. They broke through again. Coyote himself came home, out of breath with running. They all came back.

The next day he gathered the people again. They surrounded the antelope. "Run after the one that has the quiver," he told them. The antelope stood facing outward. They broke through again. The next day he gathered the people together again and they formed a circle. The antelope stood facing outward. They broke through the line. He himself was out of breath.

29. Antelopes Take Arrows from Coyote. (Second Version.)

Coyote having come to Owl who alone possessed arrows, took them away from him and killed him. After that, Coyote was the only one who had arrows and everyone was afraid of him. Since the arrows belonged to bad people, the others came together and discussed how they might take them away. The chief said to them, "That crazy fellow has the arrows. How shall we take them from him?" Black tail and white tail deer were first consulted. When it was Antelope's turn to be heard he said, "You need someone who is smart, I will take the arrow away from him for you."

Antelope's two small children went to Coyote who challenged them to a footrace. "You are too small to run a race," he replied. Beginning to run about them Coyote put the quiver on one of them and the bow on the other. When they were some distance from Coyote, they became large antelope. When Coyote realized what had happened, they were already a considerable distance away. He ran after them, but they were running very fast.

"Wait, my nephews," he called after them, "I will tell you something." The antelope paying no attention to him, ran on. Coyote became very tired. "Wait," he said, "it is my turn, give the arrows to me." "When you overtake us, we will give them to you," they replied.

Coyote having stopped, the two antelope stopped also but would not let him come near them. Coyote said, "Now, my nephews, your horns will be like bows and your manure will be like arrows."

Then Antelope said to the others, "I have taken away for you the things you were wishing, the arrows Coyote had in his hand. That is why it is good now. It Would have happened that people who were not good would have possessed arrows, and would have shot and killed human beings." Those who could run fast took away the arrows and all the other people were afraid. "You did well," the others said to them. "Now we need not be afraid." In this manner the arrows were taken from Coyote.

30. Coyote Tries to Make His Children Spotted

[1]

A deer was going along the arroyo among the willows with her spotted fawns. Coyote, coming up to her, said, "How do you make your little ones so spotted?" "Why, they are born that way," she told him. Coyote did not believe it. "O no, you do something to them to make them that way." Then Deer said, "I dig a hole for them at the top of the ridge where the wind blows up, then I pile a lot of cedar wood in front, and set it on fire. The sparks that fly out make them spotted." "What did I tell you?" he said.

He went home after his children and said to them, "Come my little children, I will make you spotted." He made a hole for them on the crest of the ridge where the wind blows up. He piled cedar wood in front of the opening, lit it, and then sat at one side to watch. They climbed over each other, crying, until the fire killed them. When the fire had burned down he looked at them. When he saw their lips turned back and their teeth showing in white rows he said. "O, you are laughing because you are so beautifully spotted." He took one of them by the arm, but when he pulled, it came off. They were thoroughly cooked.

He went away to find the deer. He set the willows on fire where he supposed she was, saying, "You told me a lie. You may say, tsi." When the fire had burned out there was nothing there for the deer had gone out on the other side. Coyote started away again.

[1] Russell has this story in just the same form but it is told of Fox although the concluding sentence refers to the characteristic howl of Coyote, (a), p. 265. Compare, Stevenson, p. 153.

31. Coyote Kills His Own Child Instead of The Turkeys

[1]

Coyote came where a flock of turkeys was rolling in the dust. He put them in a sack, saying, "I am going to roll with you." When he had rolled with them twice he carried them home. He told his children to build a fire and then said, "You had better consider what we will do with them." The smallest child said, "We should take them out of the sack one at a time, wring their necks, and put them in the fire." Another one proposed that they should all break off sticks for clubs and stand in a circle about the fire where all the turkeys could be turned loose. This they did. The youngest coyote rushed in where the turkeys were scattering the ashes, with their wings and he only was killed. "Why only the little one, the smartest. is dead." Coyote started away again.

[1] Dorsey, (d), p. 102; (a), p. 458.

32. Coyote and Porcupine Contend for A Buffalo

[1]

Porcupine was sitting where the buffalo trail crossed a stream. "Take me across," he said to Buffalo. "All right, sit between my horns," said Buffalo. "When you shake your head I shall fall into the water," said Porcupine. "Well, sit in the middle of in my back," said Buffalo. "When you shake yourself I shall fall into the water," said Porcupine. "Sit by the root of my tail, then," Buffalo said. "When you shake your tall, I shall fall," he said. "Well then, crawl inside of me," said Buffalo. Porcupine crawled inside and crossed the river. He gnawed off a large blood vessel and Buffalo fell with him at the edge of the water. Porcupine crawled out.

"I will look for a flint to butcher it with," Porcupine was saying to himself when Coyote came by and heard him. "What did you say?" asked Coyote. "I will look for a small flint with which I can make an arrow I was saying." "You said something good," Coyote replied, "'I will look for a flint to butcher it with' you were saying. Let us go where it is." They went there. "Let the one who jumps over it butcher all of it," Coyote suggested. When Porcupine tried to jump over it he fell against its belly. Coyote jumped over its tail and commenced to butcher it, while Porcupine watched him. When Coyote had finished he gave the intestines to Porcupine saying, "Wash them for me." Porcupine ate some of them after he had washed them. When he returned with them, Coyote being suspicious, looked into his mouth and saw remnants of the food. He killed Porcupine with a club. He lay there dead.

Coyote, having defecated by the Buffalo, started home for his children. When he had gone a little way Porcupine jumped up. Coyote's faeces called out, "He has jumped up." Coyote came back and killed Porcupine with his club. When Coyote had gone some distance again, Porcupine jumping up, threw dirt into the mouth of the faeces as they were about to shout the warning. They did not shout again.

Porcupine carried the meat to the top of a pine tree, and sat down there to eat it. When Coyote came back with his children there was no meat there. They just licked up the blood. Porcupine, sitting up in the tree, spoke to them, "Lie down under the tree, cover yourselves with a blanket and I will throw down some meat." They all lay down but the youngest one watched Porcupine through a hole in the blanket. "He is throwing the backbone at us," he cried and jumped up. The backbone fell on them and killed them, all except the smallest one.

"Climb up Porcupine. called to the remaining one. He climbed the tree and Porcupine gave him the neck glands of the buffalo. When he had eaten them he asked Porcupine where one might ease himself. "Where the slender limb projects one sits," he replied. When the little Coyote had gone there Porcupine kicked the branch so that he fell into the canyon and burst.

[1] Russell, (a), p. 263; Lowie, (a), p. 267; Mason, P. 316; Kroeber, (c), p. 270; Spinden, p. 21.

33. Coyote Loses His Eyes

[1]
Coyote took out his eyes and threw them up. They fell back again. Some time after, when he was walking through the woods and happened to be under a tree, he did this. His eyes caught on the tree. He went away again in this direction. Someone made eyes for him out of yellow pitch and cautioned him, "You must not lie in the sunshine." Coyote, however, did lie in the sunshine and the pitch when it became warm ran down on each side of his nose. That is the reason Coyote has marks from each eye down his checks. The eyes that Coyote threw into the tree became plums. [2]

[1] Matthews' account obtained from the Navajo has considerable detail, pp. 89-91. This story has wide distribution: Teit, (b), p. 632; Russell, (b), p. 215; Wissler and Duvall, p. 29; Kroeber, (a), p. 70; (b), p. 168; and p. 50; Mason. p.314; Stevenson, p. 153.
[2] This sentence was obtained at the end of text 35, out of its connection.

34. Coyote Kills the Prairie Dogs

Coyote tied the long hair from a buffalo's leg to a stick making it look like a scalp and started off, carrying it in his hand. When he came to a prairie dog town he told them to shut their doors and come and dance. They did so. Coyote had a stone concealed in his hand with which he hit the prairie dogs, killing them as they danced round in a circle. He told them that it was the dancing that killed them and that toward evening they would get up again. The smallest of the prairie dogs who was being carried on his mother's back called out, "He has a stone in his hand." At this, all the prairie dogs ran toward their houses which, being closed, they were unable to enter. Coyote striking at them on both sides had killed a good many.

Then Coyote brought them all together and built a large fire. When it had burned down he separated the ashes and put in the prairie dogs to cook, putting the smallest one across the others at the top. Having arranged them, he covered them with ashes and built a fire on top. While they were cooking he went to sleep. Wildcat, coming along, took all the prairie dogs out. He removed their tails, putting them back in the ashes, and replaced the little one on top. He carried all the remainder away with him and commenced to eat them.

When Coyote woke up he took a stick and poked out one of the prairie dogs. Seeing that it was small he said, "O, I do not need this one," and threw it away. It fell into the top of a tree which stood close to a stream of water. Coyote then seized a tail and pulled it out. "O, the tail has burned off." He then poked around with a stick in vain. There were none.

He went to find the one he had thrown away. Seeing it lying, as he supposed in the water, he dived and searched for it in vain. When he came out of the water he saw it still lying there. He did this four times and then lay down by the edge of the water to rest. On looking up he saw it in a tree above him. Jumping up, he got it and chewed it up bones and all. [1]

[1] A very similar story is told of Old Man by the Blackfoot, Wissler and Duvall, p. 29.

35. Coyote Is Revenged on Wildcat

[1]

Coyote started off to find Wildcat. He came upon him while he was sleeping. Having built a fire he took out Wildcat's rectum and cooked it. When it was done he woke Wildcat and showing him the morsel, said, "This is all your people gave me to eat, although they have been killing plenty." He gave the piece to Wildcat who began to eat it. When there was little left, he told him the source of the food. Wildcat put back the small part that remained. That is why the fat of Wildcat is spotted.

[1] Mrs. Stevenson has the incident in greater detail from the Sia, p. 148.

36. Coyote and Beaver Play Tricks on Each Other

[1]

Coyote, as he was traveling, came to the shore of a large lake where he lay down and went to sleep. Beaver coming there, took him out to the center of the lake where he woke him up. Coyote started to swim to the shore but when he had gone a little way, gave it up, and came back. Beaver, swimming around him, forced him toward the shore. Coyote continued to turn back and Beaver to force him on, until he finally reached the shore where he came out of the water nearly dead.

He walked along keeping watch until he found Beaver sleeping on the shore of the lake. Coyote, taking him on his back, carried him far from the water where he woke Beaver. Beaver started back to the water, hitching himself along. Coyote kept running about him as he crawled along. When Beaver got back to his home, he was nearly dead and had the skin all worn from his hands.

[1] This statement lacks connection. The full story explains the shortening of Wildcat's nose and the lengthening of Coyote's, the one operating on the other while sleeping.

37. Coyote Apes His Hosts

[1]

Coyote while traveling, came to a rock standing close to the water's edge where Kingfisher had his home. Kingfisher in greeting him said, "You have come to me when there is nothing to eat." Right below him there was smooth ice over the water into which Kingfisher nevertheless jumped and brought out a fish for his guest. Coyote ate it and when he took his leave said, "Come and see me."

Coyote camped in a place where a rock was standing. When Kingfisher came to see him, Coyote greeted him, saying, "You have come to see me when there is nothing to eat." There was smooth ice right below into which Coyote jumped, striking his nose so hard that he died. His guest took a fish out of the water for him and brought him to life. Giving the fish to Coyote he said, "I have magic power for this sort of thing." When Coyote had eaten it, Kingfisher went home.

As he was traveling Coyote came where Buffalo's wife was fleshing a hide. Buffalo greeting him said, "You have come to us when there is nothing to eat." After a time, putting his hand behind him, he brought it back with some meat. Having pounded it up fine, he pushed a stick up each of his nostrils from which fat ran down on the meat. Having mixed the food, be gave it to Coyote on a dish to eat. As Buffalo was eating he kept saying, "Whu u," Coyote was afraid and jumped up. "O, I always make that sort of noise," said Buffalo. This happened four times, Coyote being afraid each time. "Come to see me," said Coyote as he took his leave.

When Buffalo came to see Coyote he found him at his home wrapped in a buffalo robe and wearing horns which he had made for himself. Ills wife was fleshing a hide. "You come to us when there is nothing to eat," Coyote said to Buffalo. He took some bark from under his blanket and pounded it up. When he pushed a stick up his nostrils only blood dropped on the meat. "What was it I did wrong?" he said. Buffalo put his hand behind himself, took out some dried meat, and pounded it up for him. He pushed a stick into his nostrils and fat flowed out which he mixed with the meat. Passing it to Coyote he said, "Eat it, I have magical power for this sort of thing."

Coyote traveled along and cattle where Elk was lying. He was a large elk with many branched horns. Elk greeting him said, "You have come to us when there is nothing to eat." When Elk turned his head sideways, Coyote was afraid and jumped. "O, I am always this way. Do not be afraid," said Elk. Reaching to his hip he took off a piece of meat and gave it to Coyote who ate it. Coyote as he left said, "Come and see me."

When he came to Coyote's home, he was lying there with sticks pointing in different directions, tied to his head. His face was all swollen. "You come to us when there is nothing to eat," he said. After a time, Coyote put his hand under his blanket and took out some pine bark which he gave him. "What did I do wrong?" he said. Then Elk, taking out some meat, gave it to him. "I do this by magical power," he said, "eat it." Coyote, ate it.

Coyote traveling this way, came where a bird [2] had its home. This bird had red feathers which he spread out. Coyote being afraid, said, "Your house is on fire." "O, I am always this way," said the bird. "Come and see me," said Coyote, as he left.

When he cattle to Coyote's house it was burning. Coyote had set fire to it. "Your house is on fire," said the guest. "O, I am always that way"' said Coyote. The fire had burned close around him but Coyote giving his tail a flap jumped over it. [3]

[1] Russell has an additional incident with Prairie Dog as host, (a), p. 265. Matthews has given a similar story in which Wolf was host, p. 87. Compare similar stories, Lowie, (a), p. 265; Dorsey and Kroeber, 113-120; Kroeber, (c), p. 264.
[2] One of the woodpeckers.
[3] Among the Caddo, Coyote puts fire on his head to imitate woodpecker, Dorsey, (d), p. 94.

38. Coyote is Disobeyed by Turkey

[1]
Coyote came where there was a flock of turkeys. He said to one of them, "Go to my home and they will eat you. Tell them that they must save the hind quarter that has a black mark on it for me." Turkey went to Coyote's home and said to his family, "Coyote says that you should eat the smallest child, but that you shall mark a hind quarter and save it for him. That was what your father told me when he sent me to you." Coyote's wife struck the youngest child on the side of his head and killed him and then they ate him up.

Turkey went back to the people. When Coyote came back he said, "Where is that man I sent you to eat?" "When he came to us, he said, 'Your father sent me here to tell you that you should kill the smallest child and eat him, saving the right hind quarter marked with a coal for me., Because of that we killed the smallest child and ate him. The right hind quarter we marked with a coal and put away for you," they told Coyote. "May he die! He lied. I sent him to you that you should eat him."

Coyote started away again and cattle to the turkeys. They flew away from him and alighted in a pine tree. Coyote started to chop down the tree. When it was about to fall, they flew off to another tree which Coyote also commenced to chop. As it was about to fall they flew again into still another tree. This Coyote also cut down. Before it fell, the turkeys flew, alighting in still another tree. Coyote commenced chopping this also. Before it fell, the turkeys flew away alighting in another tree. Coyote tired out, gave up the task. [2]

[1] The Wichita story has Coyote first make Turkey declare he is an honest man, Dorsey, (b), p. 289.

[2] Ed. Ladd added that Coyote shot his arrows into the under side of the limb on which the turkeys were sitting in a row, cut the tree down and recovered his arrows. He repeated this four times.

39. Coyote Is Shot with A Pine Tree

[1]

A long time ago, Coyote was traveling about. He came where a small brown bird was feathering arrows. He was putting feathers on the trunk of a whole pine tree that stood there. "That arrow will not kill anything. Let me see it," said Coyote. "Shoot me with it." They shot him with it. He ran away from them and everybody ran after him. Finally, Coyote was tired out. The arrow had passed through him carrying away all of his body except a rim of hair. "The hair on my back must have blown off," Coyote said.

[1] Kroeber, (a), p. 69; Dorsey and Kroeber, p. 54.

40. Coyote Insults the Rock

[1]

Coyote ran off from there and came where a rock was rolling around under a cliff. "I am going to roll over you," the rock said. "I run fast. You can not run over me," said Coyote. "Don't say that, I will roll over you," cried the rock. Coyote defecated and urinated on top of it. The stone commenced to roll. Coyote was running around in front of it. "Here I am, roll on me," he cried. It was rolling after him pretty fast. Coyote, as he was running around, started up a hill. The stone came after him. When he started down, the stone still came after him. For a long time, they did that until Coyote was tired out. "I am going to clean it," said Coyote. Then he licked it clean and started off again.

[1] Dr. Lowie secured a more extended form among the Northern Shoshone. Lowie, (a), p. 262. Compare Dorsey and Kroeber, p. 65; Mason, p. 306; Kroeber, (c), pp. 260-264; Dorsey, (c), p. 260.

41. Coyote Marries Under False Pretences

He came to a camp and asked that a girl be given him in marriage. The man had said, "I will give my daughter to one who has large leg muscles." Coyote, displaying his leg muscles, was given the girl. A horse whinnied. "That is my horse, making the noise," Coyote said. After they had stayed there sometime they prepared to move the camp. "I am going to get my horse," Coyote told them. His wife's family still remained there while the others moved away. When Coyote did not return, those who remained started and went to the other camp. "My horse came this way," said Coyote, as he ran out toward them. "A panther skin saddle blanket was on him and the halter and bridle of rope were dragging." [1]

[1] A panther skin saddle blanket is an affectation of the wealthy.

42. Mosquito Marries Under False Pretences

Coyote ran off again from them. They did not find him and went off camping in another direction. The man married his daughter to Mosquito. He came to her at night. Early in the morning he said, "I am going to hunt," and went off. At night he came back bringing nothing but the blood. "I will go after the meat in the morning," he told them. He came back at night without anything, saying, "The ravens ate up all the meat." "Why did not you bring the bones, at least?" they asked. "The bones too, were all chewed up," he replied. The next evening he came back bringing nothing but blood. "I put the meat in a tree," he told them. The next day he went after it but came back reporting that the ravens had eaten it all. "Well, why did not you bring the bones anyway?" they asked him. "The bones too, were all eaten up," he said. While they were still sleeping the sun came up. His wife uncovered his face. His mouth was slender and very long. His arms and legs were very slender too. She stood and looked at him. They took the tipi down and moved it. When he woke up he covered his head with his blanket and went off in this direction. She left him.

43. Coyote Deceives A Woman

They moved their camp from that place. Another girl became Coyote's wife. "I am going off to hunt," he said, and went away. At evening, when he came back his face and hands were covered with blood. He had caused his nose to bleed and rubbed the blood on his face and hands. "I killed a good many of them," he told them. "I am going to get the meat," he said next morning and started back toward it. He came home without anything. He had just been telling lies.

44. Coyote and The Mexicans

One time, they say, they caught Coyote for his lying and put him in a sack. They started to carry him to California, where the judge lived. They brought him to the house of the judge. Coyote turned himself into a girl. The judge removed his clothes with the intention of spending the night with the girl. When he opened the bag Coyote came out and began to bite him. The judge ran out crying. Coyote taking all the money started to carry it home. Whenever he came to a tree he threw money on it.

He came where a Mexican lived who had treated his dog badly. it was very poor. "Compadre," Coyote said, "how is it you are so poor?" "Compadre," replied the dog, "my people treat me badly." "I will make them treat you well," said Coyote. The Mexican had some hens. "I will run off with one of the hens," said Coyote. Then Coyote seized one and ran off with it, biting it as he ran along slowly. "Where is the dog?" said the Mexican. Then he sent the dog after Coyote who was now beyond the hill. The dog ran up to him, took the hen and carried it back. On that account they treated the dog well.

The family went off to a dance one night leaving the dog at home. Coyote came to see him. "Compadre, are you staying all by yourself?" asked Coyote. The dog replied, "I am just by myself, Compadre." They were staying there together when Coyote asked the dog, "What is in that box?" "There is a bottle of whisky in there," said the dog. "Compadre, let us take a drink," Coyote said. They took out one bottle and began to drink it. When they finished the bottle Coyote said, "Compadre, I am going to shout." "Don't do it," said the dog, "the people might know about it." Nevertheless, Coyote became drunk and commenced to shout. The people came back, whipped the dog and drove him out. Coyote had defecated on all the clothes. That is why the dresses of the Mexican girls are spotted. The trees upon which he threw the money became apple trees. That is why apples are sold for money.

[1] This is a Mexican folk tale which is told in Spanish by the Mexicans in New Mexico.

45. How Mole Won the Race

All the men congregated to run a race to the border of the world where a pretty girl was living. The one who would get there first would marry her. They were running, along, Coyote far ahead of all the others. He kept looking back as he ran along. The men were all running one behind the other.

Heron started to run long after the others had set out. He ran by all the others as they were going along a slope, and came where Mole was running throwing a lot of dust over himself. "Where are you running?" said Heron to Mole. "We are all running to that girl over there." "Sit on my back," said Heron to Mole. He lay by Heron's tail who ran with him passing everyone else. Finally, he came where Coyote was by himself, far ahead of the others. He turned and looked back. Heron passed by him and coming near the place put Mole down saying to him, "Hurry up now, run." Mole came there. When Coyote and the other men came running along, Heron said to them, "What are you running for? Mole has already married the girl."

46. Frog Wins from Antelope in A Footrace

[1]

Two antelope were gambling with a white tailed deer and a frog. The antelope and deer ran a race in the woods. White tail deer jumped over the tree and beat, for antelope had to run where there are no trees. He won from antelope the dew claws and the fat on the hips.

Then the antelope suggested that they run a race with frog out on the plains. Many frogs put themselves in a line, reaching from the starting place to the goal. When they started to run each frog jumped this way just as one shakes a string. The antelope was beaten because he thought frog could not possibly win. That was the way it was done.

[1] The story is told of Coyote and Turtles among other tribes. Dorsey, (d), p. 105; (e), p, 143.

47. When the Birds Were Chiefs

They made Robin chief they say. When he spoke as a chief all the clouds disappeared. Then after him Tsîtc'ike spoke as chief. Then everybody killed game and his people were well pleased, and next Tcogaligo was chief. They had very much deer meat and his people were pleased. All the people were bringing meat and were happy because of their chief.

When TcîL [1] became chief and spoke it grew cold. "Do not speak," they said to him or it will snow. "Go and eat cedar fruit," they said to him, "you have talked enough." "Let me alone anyway, I am the chief. Do not bother me," he said to them. "Wherever I camp, the heat almost kills me. My children cry because of the heat. Because my mouth is cold I do not live among the people. I go about by myself, whistling. I ask that much snow should fall on you because you do not like me. That is why I do not like you. If you do not bother me my mind is not against you." Thus he spoke, they say.

[1] A brown bird big as a robin.

48. Woodpecker Describes Himself

They say Woodpecker spoke as follows: "I like to climb trees. I live among them because no one talks to me. I peck holes and eat with my hard bill. I raise my children in the holes I make. That is why I like the trees. I live upon their pitch. Whatever happens I do not complain because I have supernatural power. I like to carry about the rotten pine. I like to pull off its bark. I like the trees because I live upon them. He painted my face red and made my bill with which I carry wood. Although I peck with it all day, my head does not ache. My hand does not get tired because I am used to it. I go among the trees all the time because I like them very much. I eat the pitch and get fat from it. I go among the trees by means of my wings. I like to fly about from the top of one tree to another. That is why I do not complain. Because it is my nature I live among the trees. I sleep well in my house."

49. Flicker Describes Himself

"My name is Gose 'flicker.' I eat with my long bill. I fly with my wings which are red underneath. My legs are blue and the borders of my eyes are pinkish. My voice is loud and when I sing all the people hear me. They like my voice. This is my nature," he said they say.

50. Lewis Woodpecker Describes Himself

"My name is Niji. My eyes shine. My beads are becoming to me and my coat is very black. I raise my children in a hole in a tree. My young like to live there. They feed upon grasshoppers and flies. I live with my children. My red breast is becoming to me. I shout every summer and the people like to hear me. They all know my voice. I do not eat much pitch but I like acorns." This way he spoke they say.

51. Owl Describes Himself

"I am called Yî, 'owl'. I carry a basket and frequent the low gaps looking for people. I sing for them but do not think about them." "If you come to see me, you may eat the leg which lies in the basket," he told him. "There is nothing in it," his guest replied. "Yes, there is pemmican in it," he said. "That is my luncheon. When the sun goes down my basket will be full of meat."

"Where shall I come to see you?" he asked. "You may come to me where the two cedars stand." He came there at evening and found his friend with a basket full of meat. The pemmican that had been in it was gone. "This is something's meat; take it home to your children." Then he carried it to his children. "I am carrying it home to my children," he said. "There are not many of them, there are only two." "Any way I am pleased, for I was looking for provisions. My children eat nothing but meat. They become large quickly because there are only two of them." "The people fear me because of my eyes. They are afraid also of my yellow horns. This is my nature. I bring you people's meat and I say to him, 'whu o whu!'" Thus he spoke they say.

52. Panther, The Great Hunter

When Panther hunts they say he kills many deer. He only kills the big bucks. His house is full of buckskin. He only eats the hind quarters and the breast. His wife dresses hides until she is tired and then calls her daughter to help. "I told you to rub this skin. You are lazy about it," she said to her.

The trees about his house were about to break with the drying meat. Wolf came to visit them. He gave him a hind quarter when he came to his tent. People's fat is good. He pounded the meat for him and gave it to him. "Have you satisfied your hunger, my partner?" he inquired.

"Thanks, my friend, I have had enough." When he went home his children ate of the meat and were happy. "I do not want anything," his wife said, "I am satisfied. My husband goes hunting and comes back with meat."

"That is the way I do," said Wolf. "I kill nothing but bucks for you. I began by killing fawns but now I don't shoot them. You shall eat nothing but hind quarters. You shall be wiping the fat from your mouth. When I start out to kill I succeed. There is plenty of buckskin in my house. You will see plenty of deer meat there and you will get tired of carrying it. You will be tired of carrying meat by the time I have hunted twice. You may rely on me for I do it for you. No one comes to me and asks for meat in vain."

53. The Governor, Old Woman White Hands

Long ago, four men lived at Taos lying on a shade. [1] They went about with their minds but their bodies remained at Taos. One of them went east looking for the enemy and found their camp. The four men came there and took their stand facing inward from the four directions. They killed the enemy, driving them in toward the center. They killed the enemy but burned up their property. After this they would come back to Taos and lie on the shade.

One went east again and found the enemy camped on this side of the Arkansas at Tsekûî?aye, "rock stands up". He came back and reported. They sent him to Santa Fé, saying, "Go to Old-woman-her-hand-white and tell him to kill the enemy for us. Tell him to come at once."

The messenger came to the governor and told him. The governor did not believe the man but put a ball and chain on his ankle to roll along as he walked.

He did not return at the end of the first day or the second. "May you die! Old-woman-white-hands you have done something to him. That is why be does not come back," they said. The next day he did not come although they expected him. "May you die! You must have done something to Okadî. Now, we had better go after him," they said. When they came there they asked, "Where is the man we sent to you asking that you kill the enemy for us?" Then Okadî came there from the jail walking very slowly, the ball tied to him rolling along. They looked at him and said, "His father was good to him and made a rattle for him." "You had better unfasten the chain. This is the man who came to tell you to kill the enemy for us," one of them said to the governor.

After two days they said, "Hurry and get ready. We will go back to Taos and wait there for you."

They gave them horses fitted out with bells. They started back, the bells sounding sîs.

They said again, "Oh, his father was good to him. He travels with the bells jingling." They carne there and gave the horses and bells to the Pueblo Indians and then went upon their shade.

They remained there one day and then the next saying, "May you die! What is Old-woman-white-hands doing while another day passes?" And then over there the dust was rising from the horses as they came. They came to Taos with their horses all sweaty and camped by the sinking place.

At evening, they came to see them saying, "Old-woman-white-hands, where shall we camp to-morrow?" "Close by," he told them. "Oh, you must be with child," they told him. "We will start early to-morrow and get there before you," one of them said.

They were already there eating in the evening when the others rode up with sweaty horses. After dark, they came to the governor's camp and said, "Now, Old-woman-white-hands, where shall we camp to-morrow?" "Not far," he replied. "You must be with child if you can't go farther than that, Old-woman-white-hands," they said. "We will start early to-morrow ahead of you."

They were sitting there, eating, about sunset when the others rode up with sweating horses. They went to him in the evening, saying, "Old-woman-white-hands, where shall we camp to-morrow?" "Not far," he replied. "Oh, Old-woman-white-hands, you must be with child. A little farther than that," they told him. "We will start early to-morrow ahead of you."

They were sitting there eating already. "You had better go and look at the enemy again," they told Okadî who was their servant. He went and looked. "Their camp is all quiet yet," he reported. They moved toward them. When they were near they told him again, "You had better go and look again. We will wait until evening." When they were near the enemy's camp they built a fire. "Now, Okadî, go to the enemy and get something to eat."

He went there where they were eating and they gave him some meat. The four men were sitting eating. "Go again and get water," they told him. He went there again and borrowed a water basket with which he brought them water. When they had drunk they said, "Carry the water basket back to your enemy." He carried it back.

The four men lay down. The others came about daybreak the next morning. They moved toward the enemy who had their camp on either side of an arroyo. The next day the men stood facing from the four directions. The enemy discovered them. They began to kill the enemy with their war clubs. They had no arrows but just clubs for weapons. On the other side of the arroyo they were not fighting. They fought with those on the one side until they were all killed. They went among those who had not fought, saying, "These are my folks," and stroked their hair as a sign of friendship. They gathered up all the personal property and the horses. "Now, Old-woman-white-hands, tell your people to stand in line on the other side," one of them told the governor. They distributed the goods among them.

Then he said to those of the enemy with whom he had made friends, "Pick out your horses." They picked them out.

"Now, Old-woman-white-hands, give the other horses to your people," he told the governor. When the horses had been given out be said to the governor, "Now, Old-woman-white-hands, you may camp after us as short marches as you wish. You have become a rich man. Go back as slowly as you wish." The four men went back from there in one day and climbed up to the top of their shade.

[1] The common four-posted raised platform on which food is stored and under which the family often sits.

Traditions and Personal Experiences

54. The War with The Americans

Long ago, the Jicarilla were camping at Mora. A large band was also camping on the Canadian. There were many cattle about there, one of which was wearing a bell. This one the Apache killed. They were discovered and the American soldiers came, demanding four chiefs. The Jicarilla would not give them up. The soldiers rode back and the Jicarilla moved their camp to another place. The soldiers came again on horseback and demanded the four chiefs. Before the fight began, the Americans passed about their canteens and drank whisky, becoming drunk. They then rode toward the Apache shooting at them. Their fire was returned, three of the Americans being killed. One Apache had his finger shot off.

The Jicarilla moved their camp to a mountain east of Picuris. When they had been there four days the Americans came again on horseback early in the morning. They halted and one approached to pass the Apache a paper. An Apache took it from the hands of the officer and tore it up. Someone shot the person who had handed the paper, wounding him in the arm. Then the soldiers opened the fight. They had halted on the plain with their horses and were shooting in different directions, the Indians having surrounded them. The Apache kept on shooting and killing the soldiers until only two were left. Four of the Apache were killed. They took all the arms of the soldiers and the money from their clothes, a large sum.

From there the Apache moved to the west side of the Rio Grande. From there they moved to El Rito and afterward to Vallecitos. A company composed of Mexicans, Pueblos, and soldiers, followed them, shooting at the Indians who moved their camp without anyone being killed. They camped by Coyote from which place turning back they went to Conejos. From there they moved eastward to Saikanyedîye on top of the mountain. From there they went to the branch of the Arkansas near Pike's Peak and Pueblo. They then moved eastward to a canyon where they mingled with the Ute. They rode down to a place where a Mexican was living, killing all the people that were there. They brought back a scalp and danced with it.

After about a month they moved eastward from Pueblo where they encountered a large number of the enemy. The fighting began early in the morning. The Apache climbed to the top of the mountain on foot where they remained for some time and then went westward coming to DziLdîLee. After camping there a few days they continued westward. Again a band of soldiers, Mexicans and Pueblo Indians commenced to fight them. The Ute withdrew from the Apache who broke up into small bands and scattered in different directions. The Ute, not wishing to continue fighting, went to the various Mexican towns where they lived.

The Apache stayed in the mountains where the enemy, Mexicans, Pueblos, and American soldiers joined in fighting them as if they had been deer. Many old women and children died of starvation. Leaving the country east of Conejos, the Apache came to the neighborhood of Pagosa, camping among the mountains at the head waters of the Chama. At Tierra Amarilla, they joined the camp of a band of Ute. After remaining there a while, they moved their camp to Cangillon near Abiquiu. There the American soldiers made peace with them, distributing goods from wagons. Each Indian received a present and peace was established. "Are these all there are left of you?" asked one of the Americans. "Yes, only so many," replied an Apache. "You were nearly exterminated," said the American. "Do not become enemies again. Many old men, children, and women, have died," he said. [1]

[1] Casa Maria said that when this happened he was about as old as his youngest deaf mute son, about twelve or fourteen. He said the American general's name was Gidi who afterward died at Taos. He agreed that this was probably the man called by Americans, Kit Carson. He said that the goods were issued by a man named Baixahi. In the Annual Report of the commissioner of Indian Affairs for 1855, Mr. Merriweather, governor and superintendent of Indian affairs in New Mexico reports both the expedition and the making of peace. The presence of St. Vaian, an officer or the New Mexican volunteers, is mentioned. In the same report (p. 192) Mr. Carson mentions the fact that he was present at the time peace was made. An extended account of this war is given in the, "Life and Adventures of Kit Carson," Peters, pp. 414-526.

55. The Horses of the Apache Are Stolen by The Navajo

Their camp was there at Cimarron. In the springtime the Navajo came and drove their horses away. The Apache rode after them, mounted on their horses which the Navajo had failed to get. As they followed them they found the poorer horses standing one by one. They brought only these home with them. When it was fall the Ute and Apache together went after them where they had driven the horses away. At KôLtsõye, "yellow river" they drove away the horses of some Mexicans. There they saw two mules which they took away and hid in the brush. From there they went to Bosque where all the Navajo had been placed. [1] When they got there, six Ute rode on in front and after dark drove away four of the horses. Two of the Ute, who were out after another horse during the night, came upon a Navajo whom they shot, inflicting a flesh wound. The Navajo hid in the brush and the Ute brought back only the horse with the saddle.

Early the next day they rode toward them. The soldiers were drawn up on horseback in front of the ditch where the Apache and Ute dismounted and went forward with a flag which they had raised. The soldiers then announced that they would fight against whichever tribe fired the first shot. They then rode with them into the town of Bosque. The Ute and Apache rode in the middle with the soldiers on each side. The Navajo, coming up, said bad words against them but the soldiers surrounding the Apache would not let the Navajo attack them. Even when they were inside, the Navajo came up, still wishing to fight. Finally, they gave it up. Two soldiers stood by the door watching while the Indians were eating. A Navajo who wanted to sell something came up behind the soldiers and attempted to go in. The soldiers, discovering him, shot him right there and killed him. His own people (Navajo) took him outside.

After remaining there four days the Ute and Apache started home not having been given their horses because they had already stolen others.

Some of the enemy had been to Santa Fé. One of the family had died. If any other tribe finds us, let them kill us if they want to," they said. They came to Santa Fé, two men, two women, and four children, eight of them altogether. As they were coming back from Santa Fé toward evening, the Apache and Ute returning from there (Bosque) saw them. Riding after them, they overtook them and commenced to fight. They killed one man. Two rode off and one woman attempted to escape on foot, favored by the darkness. They caught three of the children and this woman. The, y also captured the horses with their packs in which they were taking home, corn, bread, flour, peas, and whisky. They brought them all away, arriving after night where the Apache were camped. They did not take the scalps because no one knew how. The Ute knew how to take scalps but the Ute did not kill him. For that reason he was not touched. [2]

Early next morning, a man went over to the Ute and told them. "You come and scalp the man. We do not know how," he said to them. They immediately commenced to shout and run after their horses. Whoever got there first jumped on his horse without a saddle, and raced to the place where the man lay. They took the scalp, and cut off the ears. They cut off the fingers too. They brought these back to their camp. One of them took the scalp, turned it over his knee, and cut off pieces of flesh. They put these pieces in the fire, eating some of them and rubbing the others on their bodies. [3]

They rode off, stopping at noon, to eat. They built a fire. A man leaned his gun against a rock. While they were eating, a Ute climbed to the top of this rock, sat down and began to sing and shout. Without anyone touching it, the gun went off, shooting this man through the hip. He fell down and the others all ran up to him. The ball passed through the bone breaking it. They moved away from there, placing the wounded man on poles fastened on each side of a horse. They dragged him along this way. [4]

They moved to Cimarron. As they rode near they held the enemy's scalp. They went dancing around there and kept it up until night. They stopped at night and the men went to their homes. Early the next morning they started dancing again, continuing until dark. They stopped to eat. The next morning they danced again, continuing until sunset. They stopped to eat but began right away to dance again. It dawned while they were still dancing. After it was daylight they commenced dancing again, stopping to eat when it was night. They commenced dancing again and continued until it was daylight when they finished.

[1] The Navajo were prisoners of war at Ft. Sumner, Bosque Redondo, on the Pecos River from 1863 until 1867.
[2] The informant commented, "Very few of the Apache know how to take a scalp. if they do not know how, it (scalping) makes them die without sickness. The body dries up. They sometimes fall in the fire."
[3] Because the enemy (Plains Indians) sometimes took off the Utes' ears and fingers to wear, the Ute did the same. "Just the Ute did this way, (ate it). The Ute say if they do this the enemy will not be strong. They will get scared quickly."
[4] The travois seems to have been used only for the transportation of the wounded and infirm, the practice of packing the loads on the backs of the horses having been adopted from the Mexicans.

56. A Fight with The Enemy on The Arkansas River

The Apache and Ute were camping together near Cimarron. After they had held the bear dance, they moved away to the Canadian River and continued camping at "small hills", "saddle-washed-away", Carriso, "Cimarron dry", and "five peaks" until they came to a plain where there were many ponds of water. From here, they moved toward the east to the plain where many buffalo had been killed. They could not tell who had killed them. They next moved to a place on the Arkansas River called "white sands." From this camp they rode eastward looking in vain for buffalo. They found only bulls going about by themselves, one of which they killed and brought back with them.

About half the hand turned back west from this point While the others went on eastward. Another buffalo bull was found by itself and killed. East of the Arkansas River they found the track of a mule and a horse led behind, evidences of the enemy They moved their camp back toward the west to a mountain called, Tseintcincyihi.

Three men turned back to hunt deer. The enemy who had been following, discovered these hunters and riding up, took away their horses. One man hid himself successfully, another escaped through the thick brush, and the third was followed by the enemy. On this side, where a small arroyo passing through a little flat enters the larger arroyo, the enemy began shooting at him. An arrow which the Apache was holding in his hand was hit in the middle. The Apache, having dismounted, waited close by in the arroyo. He shot one of the enemy who came up close to him causing him to fall from his horse. The others, coming to the same place continued the fight, shooting the Apache in the back. He pulled out the arrow but the small flint arrow-head remained in his body. He shot again and another enemy fell from his horse. The enemy were now afraid and withdrew. The Apache went into the brush. One of the men came to the Apache camp and brought them word of what had happened. That evening, several of them rode to the place on horseback. Having spent the night in the thick brush close to the enemy, they came early the next morning to the place where the two men were still staying. They found that the stones on which the blood had dropped where the enemy had been shot from his horse, had been all turned over and the bloody grass had been pulled up and thrown into the brush.

On the top of a small hill near by, a platform had been built on which the body had been placed together with all of his personal belongings. The Apache rode close by this place. They found where the enemy had been en-camped in large numbers near the creek and had killed sheep and eaten them. The enemy had gone to the mountains on the other side of the river. The Apache turned about and started toward home.

Some of the Apache, two men, two women, and three children; seven in all, had started on in advance. They noticed some people traveling behind them and sent one of the men back to see if they were their own people. When he had ridden close enough to them he saw they were not his people. When he turned to ride away the enemy rode after him, calling to him to wait. Then he stopped his horse, took off his clothes, put on his war-bonnet and shouted to them, "Now." A chief of the enemy rode toward him. The two men, drawing their knives, and stopping their horses close together, tried to pull each other from their horses. Each stabbed the other with a knife and both were killed.

The enemy then rode up and surrounded the remaining Apache. The man kept shooting at the enemy. Although the arrows fell all about none of them hit him nor was he wounded by the bullets. After a while, he was shot in the sole of his foot. He killed many of the enemy. The enemy killed two white horses near one of which the wounded man was lying. He took off the bridle and then put it down again on top of the horse. While standing there he was killed. They were all killed except one small child whose body was not found. The enemy had taken it captive. The arms and legs of two of the children had been cut off.

When the remainder of the Apache came back to Cimarron they inquired for their relatives. Finding they had not returned, a party of eight went out on horseback and found their bodies where they had been killed. They gathered up and brought home four large bundles of arrows some of which they distributed among the Ute. The Ute said that even when several had been engaged in the fight they had never found so many arrows. [1]

[1] When asked how the information was obtained concerning this encounter Casa Maria explained that a Mescalero Indian who was with the enemy at the time, afterward told of the occurrence on a ration day. The Ute immediately killed him.

57. A Duel Between Scouts

At another time they were off on a buffalo hunt. While one man was scouting ahead for the enemy he saw one of the enemy also scouting. They came toward each other, stood some distance apart and talked by the sign language. They motioned that they should come near to each other. One of them threw his arrows on the ground and held out his empty hand. Then the other one also threw his arrows upon the ground. The enemy held up his bow toward him and put that on the ground also. The Jicarilla held up his bow and put it on the ground. The enemy drew his knife, showed it to the Jicarilla, and placed it on the ground. The Jicarilla signed that he had no knife. Then they agreed to meet in the center and to make friends. Each said that he was without weapons. They met and commenced to talk by signs. Soon they were fighting with their fists. The Jicarilla was getting tired. The enemy picked him up and commenced to carry him where his weapons were lying. The Jicarilla had a knife suspended about his neck. As the enemy was carrying him toward his weapons he thought about his knife, drew it and stabbed the enemy under his arm. He dropped him and ran for his weapons. When he was close by them he fell and died. The Jicarilla scalped him, took all his weapons, and carried them to his camp. Everyone was frightened and ran back to his own country. When they came back, they made the scalp dance with it.

58. A Captive Woman Attempts to Make Peace

A company of Ute who was traveling down the Canadian River was met near Salt River by a band of the enemy from the east. Early one morning, two of the enemy rode up to a tipi where a Ute woman was staying by herself. [1] When she started to run to the main camp the enemy rode away. Her relatives, on being told what had happened, drove up their horses and, selecting the best ones, rode after the enemy. These, whom they found to be numerous, turning, rode back toward them.

An old woman, a captive from the enemy, rode out from the ranks and spoke to them. The enemy and the Ute had stopped in two lines facing each other. The old woman, attempting to make peace, rode along the line, saying, "I came out to make peace with you." When she had proceeded about half the length of the line, and the men had agreed to make peace, those at the other end of the line began to fight.

The Ute, piling up their property close to the edge of the road, took their position behind it. Their horses were tied in the arroyo. The enemy came directly at them and they began to fight. When they were close one of the enemy fell from his horse, wounded. An Apache woman having an ax in her hand jumped upon him and although he was not yet dead, cut off both his arms with the ax. She pulled his wrist guard off and threw it upon his stomach. [2]

They began to fight again, the Ute driving the enemy forward. They captured four horses from the enemy. The Ute, mounted, rode on both sides of the enemy who were on foot, pursuing them some distance. When the Ute turned back, the enemy followed them. They sang as they marched along. When the enemy came again within shooting distance, the Ute dismounted and without moving from their position, killed all their enemies and took their scalps. They immediately broke camp and set out for Cimarron which they reached in four days. They established their camp there and held the dance.

[1] The woman was by herself because of her condition at that time. She nevertheless broke the established custom in the time of peril.

[2] This story was told to explain the giving of names to children. This old woman when she returned from the expedition, gave an account of what she had done and named the narrator, Casa Maria, then an infant, bet'ô, wrist guard. It seems to have been customary among the Apache for the women to mutilate the dead thereby preventing the warriors from losing their luck by pollution.

59. The Horses of The Ollero Are Stolen

Long ago the Ollero came to Cimarron where the Llanero were then living and said, "We are going to hunt buffalo." Maxwell, having loaned them a number of good horses, burros, and mules, they went away to the plains and camped near the Canadian River. Having camped successively at K'aixactciye, Dakûgaye, and TseLîtcî naxabîLîye "stone red hangs down" they came to Nadôstse?aLîye "where pipes are made." They had now reached the range of the buffalo but there were none there except a few who were roaming about by themselves. They caught two buffalo calves with a lasso and led them home.

Breaking camp, they traveled east to Red River, having camped on the way at Cheyenne Canyon and at NabeLtc'îdîye. Riding down the river, they came to a large herd of buffalo. Riding in among them they killed several and brought the meat back home. The next day they went again after the buffalo, securing several which they brought back. Although they now had much meat they went again, on the third day, and brought back a large quantity.

That night, after it was dark, the enemy came and drove away half of their horses. The next day when their loss had been discovered they rode after the enemy but did not overtake them. After two days, they gave up the pursuit and returned to the place where the horses were driven off. Those who had extra horses lent them to those who were without for the packing of their loads. As they went back, some of the men rode far out on each side, watching for the enemy. They discovered a band of wild horses and sent word to the main party who immediately caught their good horses and rode after them. They found the wild horses on the south side of a dry lake. The wild horses having been already surrounded noticed the men, stood looking at them for an instant and then broke away. The Indians rode after them and turned them back. Coming toward them from both directions, they caught a good many. A colt was following close behind a wild horse which a man who was chasing kept missing. Soon after, having caught another wild horse, he succeeded in catching the horse which the colt was following and when he stopped it the colt stopped also. Everyone laughed. They brought many of the wild horses back to their camp.

As they came back toward the west up Canadian River they saw wild horses again near the Salt River. Surrounding them, they caught two.

From there they came to Cimarron having camped at Nagôntt'iye, Dakûgâye, K'aixactc'îye, and at the Canadian River. The Ollero went westward to their own country, and camped near El Rito. We camped on the other side of the Rio Grande by Cimarron which was our country. The enemy used to come after us there at Cimarron but we did not come westward on that account for we were not afraid of them. We used to go to the east and fight them, Sometimes the horses gave out on the journey and had to be left behind. If any of the enemy were killed their horses were taken away. When they returned with scalps, they camped about Cimarron and danced. They always kept watch toward the east while they were dancing.

60. An Expedition to the Adobe Walls with Kit Carson

It was at Cimarron also that they started off with Gidi (Kit Carson) after the enemy. There were Ute, Apache, soldiers, and Mexicans. Four different nations went with him after the enemy. They went down the Canadian River to HweLdibade (Mexican name?) where they found the enemy. There were many tipis there. At evening, when they were approaching the camp of the enemy, men were sent out to observe. There their camp was lying some way off. The party moved on until nearly day when they saw the campfires. The horsemen, leaving the others, rode forward. There were two camps of the enemy, one above the other. All the Apache rode together and commenced to fight. They drove them from the upper camp and pursued them to the lower camp where they fought with them. Taking away their horses they fought with them until night. Many of the soldiers were killed. One Apache was killed and one was wounded in the foot. A spent ball entered his foot but did not pass through it. Another Apache received an arrow under his arm through his clothing. Many of the enemy were killed and all their tents and goods were brought home on wagons. The enemy drove them away from their lower camp. They came back to Cimarron where they danced until they were tired. [1]

[1] This account was given after an inquiry had been made of Casa Maria whether he went on the expedition. He said that he did not go but that his brother went. An extended account of this affair is given by Lieut. G. H. Pettis, "Kit Carson's Fight with the Comanche and Kiowa Indians at the Adobe Walls on the Canadian River, Nov. 25, 1864." See also, Mooney, (b), p. 314-17.

61. An Unsuccessful Expedition Led by Maxwell

[1]

Fourteen men, Apache, went from there on horseback to a place called, Tcîcgedjinye, where they slept. The next morning they started off on horseback and rode to Tcîcanye, "tree stands" where they slept. The next day they rode on to K'aiLbayeye, "brown willows" where they slept. This was on KûLtsôyeye, "yellow river". The next day they rode to Djanamîîlãye, where they slept. The next day they rode to Bosque where Maxwell lived. A great many Mexicans came there in wagons, about three hundred in all. Maxwell made war-bonnets for us of white turkey tail feathers. He also made black leggings and white shirts which he gave us.

Then they started out on the plains toward the enemy. They camped at a place called in Mexican, Alamo Mucho. At Tierra Blanca they spent the next night. The next camp was at Portales. The next night was spent at Salada. From there they went on to a lake about five miles across where they camped again. They moved from there to Dakûedîye, "no water", where they saw signs of the enemy's camp. There were many bones which had been chopped up and thrown in a pile. They moved their camp to a place where there was another lake. There too, a good many of the enemy had been camping. They found where the enemy had killed a horse by the edge of the water. A woman had died here and they had placed her below a ridge of rocks and piled up stones above her. [2] A Mexican who climbed up there took the body from the grave and then began to shout. The other Mexicans ran to the place. They took away all the clothes and began to shout. They also took many bracelets which were on her.

Then it began to snow on them so that they could not see any distance. The wind also blew and it was very cold. There was no wood and the provisions were exhausted. For two days they did not eat. We turned back from there. It was close to the country of the Texans and they were afraid of them. We came back hungry to Bosque where Maxwell lived. He killed a steer for us and gave us four sacks of flour and one of coffee. He gave a horse to one man.

We ate up all of the steer. Maxwell gave us a letter to his herders directing them to kill a fat steer for us. It was very cold. We started from there and in six days came back to Cimarron not having seen the enemy.

[1] Lucien B. Maxwell who controlled about 2,000,000 acres of land in northern New Mexico on which many Ute and Jicarilla Apache lived. Cf. Inman, Col. Henry, "The Old Santa Fé Trail," pp. 373-388.
[2] There was no timber with which a platform could be built on which the body might be placed, as was usual with the enemy. The horse had been killed because of the woman's death.

62. The Apache Meet a Texan

Long ago they moved the camp east to the plains from there own country at Cimarron. They camped at DziLtcitdjaiye "mountains stand there". From there we went to DziLntsaiye, where we secured antelope meat. They moved the camp to DziLnkelleye, "mountain flat". Then they camped at Gadjaeye where they secured only antelope. They camped at KaLdeîaye, "cedar stands". Next they camped at Sîgôlôhôye. There by a lake was a band of wild horses which they surrounded when they saw them. When the, horses discovered the men they ran away. The Indians rode around in front of them on both sides. Then riding toward them they caught twenty-three which they led home. After two days they moved the camp east to a place where there was no water. Early in the morning the next day they went to Bôndaye. There on the plains they looked in vain for buffalo.

After awhile three men were out riding on the plains. They came home about evening saying that way down stream were many of the enemy camped on the flat, They rode toward them and slept that night close by. Early the next morning two men rode toward them. They approached, riding from side to side. When they came up to the place there was no enemy but buffalo. We rode to them and killed a great many. We brought home the meat arriving after dark. On the stream above us it rained hard during the night and the water came up over us, washing away much of our property and all the meat.

A Ute riding out from this camp took horses belonging to a Texan and drove them away thinking they belonged to the enemy. They drove home seven of them. A man came riding after them on a mule. His foot slipped through the stirrup and he fell off. The mule ran with him, kicking, and dragging him back to the house, dead. Then another man came out and they gave the horses to them. He asked for other horses. "You must give me ten horses because my man was killed by his horse when he was coming after you. If you do not give them to us I am going to kill you all," he said. They gave him ten horses.

When they gave him the horses he was satisfied. "You must not bother the buffalo," he told them. "If you see anything lying about you must not touch it. Let it lie there, it belongs to someone," he said.

They moved their camp to a place called Balalolo and then to Agua Azul where they found some buffalo. They killed a few; there were not many. When the buffalo were gone they moved up Red River. There were many buffalo there. They killed many and dried the meat which they tied up in parfleches and packed on the horses. They drove the horses back up the river to El Rito Blanco, camping at Millo Agua. They crossed where they make pipes in the middle of the river. From there they moved to LîyeLdeseLîye. There the river flows over a rock. They came to the Canadian River and the next day got back to Cimarron.

63. A Ute Is Saved by His War-Medicine

Long ago, over east of Picuris, where the houses were by the river there was a medicine ceremony. There were many people there and they danced. When it was over the Apache moved their camp to the top of the mountain. Their camp was at DziLdzenadzisgaye for some time, after which they moved to Cimarron. From there they camped in succession at Mik'egojîye, "black dried lake", at Tcôncjadzôye, "small pines", at DeLdîLnîye, "cranes make a noise," at K'ekôntsôye bîjaye, "small yellow spot", and at TseLgaiye, (white rock). From there one of the Ute who had their camp at Cimarron went to the town to buy whisky in canteens.

The enemy, coming from the east, met him and he commenced to fight with them although he was alone. The Apache and the Ute knew it although they were drinking whisky. His people came to him where they were fighting on the Canadian River. Just as they came there, he was shot through the chest. He caught hold of the horse's neck and fell. Someone untied his medicine which he was wearing across his chest. The Ute spit blood and sat up. They put the medicine in his mouth four times with a spear of grama grass.

"Now fill a pipe for me," he said. They filled the pipe for him and he smoked. The blood stopped flowing. They tied a cloth around his chest. He sat there.

They went after the enemy. One was killed on the banks of the Canadian River. They continued fighting as the enemy withdrew eastward. They threw away their weapons and clothing, even their breech cloths. The Apache took much of their property including many horses and brought them back with them. They danced with the scalp.

64. Pesita Is Shot

Long ago, they came to Cimarron for rations. Pesita [1] and another Indian commenced shooting at each other without the knowledge of the other Indians. The other man was shot in the shoulder with an arrow and was killed. The Ollero came running close to Pesita's tipi from all sides. They shot at each other. Pesita was hit with a musket ball and shot through the thigh. He fell right there. They stopped shooting and the Ollero ran off west to their own country. Afterwards Pesita gave them a good horse and they made friends.

They came again for rations and fought with the Americans. One Indian was shot through the flesh of his arm and another was shot through the chest, from side to side. We surrounded the house but the American agent did not want to fight and we did not shoot at each other.

Afterward there was shooting again at the same place. One Indian was killed and another was caught and put in jail. We rode there on horseback. One man rode in front of us by himself. He rode right up where the Americans were in line. When he was near, his horse was killed and he started back on foot. They shot at him. He went slowly but was not hit. He got away from them. We rode up and surrounded them but they did not want to fight. They gave the man they had in jail back to us so we did not fight. When we had gone home the soldiers came to us and made peace.

After that, rations were issued again and the meat was being given out. He gave the bones to two men. One of them struck the Agent with the bone. [2] They shot him through the flesh of the arm. They shot there inside. Then the Agent ran into his house. After a while, the Agent came out; he had been shot in his hand. They ran toward us and we started toward them. We were going to shoot but they did not attack us.

[1] A Jicarilla about 65 years old who was the informant for several of the myths.
[2] This was Juan Julian, at one time a war chief. He was angry because he was given a bone with very little meat on it.

65. The Arrows Fail on The Hunt

In the fall they camped out in the plains for buffalo. They camped at the Canadian River, then at DzîLts'îdgaiye, "mountains stand" at LiyeLdeseLye, "saddled floated away", at Balisoye, (Mexican name?) where they came among the buffalo. The bulls that were going around in advance of the herd were killed and the meat brought back. In the evening, the chief made a speech saying, "We shall stay here two days, you should have everything ready. There are many buffalo here. After two days, in the evening, we shall move camp toward them." After two days when the sun was here in the sky they started off eastward and came to Gadjaeyi and camped below in the arroyo. During the night, the buffalo ran away from them. They kept bellowing. The next day some men rode to the top of the hill to look over the country. They came back and reported that there were buffalo in large numbers in all directions. They caught their good horses and rode them out on the plains. They rode right among them killing a great number and bringing back much meat. The next day they killed many again. Still another day they killed a good many and brought in the meat.

In the evening the chief spoke to them again. "Our arrows are all gone. If the enemy sees us, there is nothing we can do, for we have nothing to shoot with." Then they were afraid and started back with some of the meat still fresh. They were obliged to leave behind some of the flour, piling it up, taking only the sacks. They turned back, some of the men having only one arrow, others none at all, and some of them having two. That was the reason they started back while the meat was still fresh. They started early in the morning and traveled until noon when they stopped. In the evening they started again and traveled through the night although they could not see. In four days they came back to Cimarron with the meat. They set to work and made many arrows.

66. A Successful Hunt

Long ago our camp was in the mountains beyond Taos. They moved away east after buffalo. They camped at TsedaLîjînye, "stone black", at ILedzîtsôye, at Tsaiskaye, "stone cup", at Ts'ist'aye, at Tcîcnadenlaye, trees in a line", at TcîcgôdîLaneye, "stumps many", at Tsets'ôsgaiye, "stones fall down", at Xanadlîneye, "many springs", at Tsetcîtcîyadn?aye, "rough stones stick up", at Nabî?anye "a river", and at Dlestsôye, "yellow paint ".

They brought meat in there; deer, white-tail deer, and elk. They saw buffalo there also and rode to them killing them. After a while they moved east to Dîgôjye, and still farther east to K'aisîkaye, "willows stand". There they brought in deer, white-tail deer, and elk. They moved to CaLgîjîhî, camping on the side of the mountain. From there they moved to Tseîtcîcî and ÎLkînacnkaye, "gun was found", and TseLtsôdas?âye, "stone yellow stands". Turning sunwise they came back, carrying much antelope and white-tail deer meat. They were not hungry as they came back to Tsentcîncîhî ain?ahî. We went up the canyon to TsedagôLtcîye, "stones top red", to Tsedahînltcîyeye, to TseîgaLîye, "stone rattle", to Tsejîkahî?aye "stones run into the water", to Nabî?anye, to Xagagaiye, to Xanadlîneye. "springs", to Tsenasdzôdeye, "stones parallel", to Dîbenadjîlôye, "sheep lowered down", to a place down stream from TcanLãhi, "much manure". They came with the meat to Idîcl'îcîye, then to Tcîcîye, "red paint", then to Baitdzesîkaye, then to Dlecnt'ûeye, "poor paint", then to Mai?kôdjîcdjîdeye, and then they all camped by Taos at TseLãye, "stones many".

67. Hunting Elk

After that time I started to hunt on the top of a mountain. There were four tipis of us. Vicientito, Luna, myself, Victor, Juan Jose, so many there were of us. We started away hunting deer. I went in advance with two of the young men and went up to the head of the canyon at Ensenada. We had only one gun. Each boy had a horse. They found a cow and a calf which they killed and brought back to me in the evening. I killed a fawn which I brought home.

Early the next morning I started with the camp, stopping about noon. The young men went out hunting there, killing a big antelope buck. When they got back, one of them said, "I killed a big antelope buck." "Hurry up, and get it," I told him. He went out after it with a horse and brought it in. The next day I moved my camp to the top of the mountain. I went to the top of the ridge where I could look back and saw the rest coming way in the distance. I camped by the stream. When they caught up with me my wife gave them meat which they ate, feeling so happy that they shouted as they ate it.

The next day we moved the camp to the top of the mountain east of the Chama where the railroad now comes up. We camped on the mountain side. When it was night they sang for deer until midnight. I moved my camp to the top of the next hill. "I am going to camp right here," I told them. The others went off hunting. I went by myself. Luna killed two big bucks; Vicientito killed one; Juan Jose killed one; I killed three. We brought home the seven deer. The next day we moved our camp, although it was raining pretty hard, and stopped on a flat by the river.

Early the next day Vicientito said, "Hurry, get things ready." Five of us started out together on foot, going to a round-topped hill at the head of the canyon. There was a lake there from the side of which we started up the mountain. On the other side of the lake from us there was an elk. Looking this way about the lake we saw a number of them. When we ran toward them they scattered. Vicientito said, "Two of you go around the lake this way. One of you sit down there. One of you stay there and wait." It was Luna he told to stay here. He placed me in the canyon. "You stay here, he told me. I sat there. Then he said, "I am going up close to one of the elk." He started toward them and I heard two shots. He killed it. I saw the bunch that had been at the junction of the canyons running over toward me. One of them was standing in a little flat, head toward me. I shot it in the neck. It was a female. It ran this way up the hill, where there was nothing but timber through which it passed. I shot again and all the elk ran back. Without hiding I ran straight toward them. When I was near them, half way up the hill, a big elk ran after me. They stopped right there, and I shot. That one did not move and I shot again at another, the biggest one, firing at his hip. He turned back and ran toward me, one of his hind legs swinging about. Brush about four feet high was standing on both sides. I stood there with him coming right at me. When he jumped I shot him in the shoulder. As I jumped sidewise, he landed right where I had been sitting. As he passed by, the blood was flowing from his shoulder. Then the elk went toward the east where Luna was sitting. It was pretty steep right in front of him. He commenced to shoot and hit four of them. Seven of the elk ran off through the thick brush. We all came together there and commenced to butcher the elk. When we had finished butchering, we built a fire and ate some of the meat.

We went home and the next day moved our camp near that place on the edge of the mountain. We brought up all the meat and the bones. Having remained there four days, the others went to hunt along the river but I remained at home. Luna killed seven which they brought to camp. We dried much meat and carried it home with us to Tierra Amarilla. We started away immediately to Cuchilla where they were to hold a feast. For that purpose we all came there. The Pueblo Indians brought fruits there and the Mexicans came with wagons and on horseback. They had a rooster race. After the feast was over we moved camp back again to Tierra Amarilla where we and the Ute remained in separate camps.

68. A Deer Hunt

At one time I was hunting deer at Seasdzôleye, "stone light", east of Coyote. From there I moved east to Yôdabîtsîlaye, "Ute his head lies". Then I went west to Ojo (Caliente) where I found deer. There were five of us in the party. I killed many deer there. We took the meat along with us, coming east again to Spotted Mountain, half way up which I camped. Not killing any deer there we moved east again. We killed deer at that place. We camped about DzîLtcîdjaie, "mountains stand". At this place we killed a large number of deer, securing a great deal of meat which we took to the town of Kûxatcîlau, "they draw water with a rope", San Felipe. When we brought the meat there the Pueblos swallowed it all red (not cooked). We sold all the meat to them. From there we went back home. I, myself, turned back east to Cuchilla, where they were to have the feast in four days. I brought meat there. In four days they all came together and held the feast which was over in four days. They moved the camp away to Abiquiu, from there to Cangillon and next to Coyote where the camp was established.

From there with only my own tent I started away hunting. At Gallinas I killed many deer and dried the meat. I went to Coyote with the meat where my wife distributed it all to her people. Then the camp was moved to Tierra Amarilla on a hill. From there I started on a hunting trip for deer. At the head of the Chama River I came where there were deer. There were four tipis of us. I killed seven elk and a great many deer. I went back to Tierra Amarilla with the deer and the elk meat. The camp remained there.

When it was fall I went on a bunting trip for deer to Gallinas. From there I went to the top of the hill where the canyons meet at Cebolla. We found a bunch of deer there. I killed one. I went home and the next day moved the camp to that place. After two days I moved the camp east in the canyon. Then I moved to Gallinas and to a place called TsekeL, "stone flat", where I established my camp.

After some time I went away from there again camping for deer. I killed deer every day not far from the camp. I only went out a little way and killed them. I packed the meat with two horses. I camped around there killing deer all winter. While I was spending the winter there the Navajo occasionally came to visit me on horseback. They ate the meat and carried some of it home with them. All winter they ate at my camp. When it was spring I moved my camp to Tierra Amarilla. "Just once more I am going to hunt deer," I said. I went off to hunt and found deer tracks. I ran after them and killed one while they were running. Having caught up with them I started to shoot, killing ten. I brought the meat in on three pack horses. I went with it to Misaye where the Apache were camped. They all came to see me and my wife gave them meat and sinew. They came to me also for the feathers of the birds I had killed. I moved away to Cebolla and then to Tierra Amarilla.

69. Deer Hunting in The Mescalero Country

They started from Tierra Amarilla and placed their camp at Cebolla. From there they moved camp to Cangillon and from there to El Rito. Next they went to Cuchilla. From there they moved to Española. From there they moved to Santa Fe, camping on the hill east of the town. Then they moved to TseLkaihî?âye. From there they went east to a Mexican town. Then they camped at Anton Chiso. Next they stopped at Alamo Gordo. From there they moved to Bosque. From there they moved to DzeLk'ane daLkîdjîye, "mulberry trees scattered". From there they moved to Naudajehi. From there they moved to Rio Bonito where the soldiers were living. They camped right among the houses of the soldiers remaining four days. From there they removed to Carrizo where the sawmill stood. The Mescalero were camped there and we camped among them. They were drinking tiswin.

After a while a number of us started after deer together. One Mexican who had married a Mescalero, Carilla, by name, was with us. We camped right by the soldiers. They nearly caught us. Some were in front of us, among them Carilla. During the night he rode back to us and we moved camp before day, although it was raining. Two men rode up behind us telling us to hurry up. We came to a gap at the end of a mountain about daylight. A large number of people camped there. We came to a lake called Pato. Early in the morning we moved from there separating into two bodies and camped at a place where there was no water. "You look for water," he told us. We searched for water in vain. Three of us found a little water standing right in the plain. We returned to the camp to find that they had moved away from us. We followed behind them until evening. They had camped at the edge of the water by Turkey Mountain.

"To-morrow we will hunt," he said. Early the next morning before daylight, Luna and I went together a considerable distance before it became daylight. We found deer running through the timber. We separated, one going on either side, and lost sight of each other. One deer ran toward me and then ran off to a distance.

I went where trees were standing and climbed up where I could see in all directions. The deer were moving about but there was nothing that could be used for cover. Being unable to get close, with the sight at the highest notch, I shot and missed. The deer ran east and I followed them. When I got near to them as they were going slowly up the mountain I shot without having moved the sight. I did not hit them. The deer ran up the steep place to the top. Then I remembered the sight and moved it back. Close by me I heard the discharge of a gun. I sat down on top of the hill and was smoking when I looked over there and saw a deer running straight toward me. I was sitting behind some trees. When it was close to me I shot. It ran off this way and I ran after it. I found blood and over there it was lying dead. I butchered it and put the meat on a tree thinking, "I will come after it to-morrow." I went home to the camp. When I came past the arroyo there was a band of deer jumping over each other. Coming up to the edge of the rock, I shot, killing seven. I butchered them and left them right there on the ground. I ran back to the camp, got a horse, and rode back. Having tied them on the horse, I brought them home.

The others also brought back meat from different directions. Luna had killed five; three antelope, two deer. Another man killed one, another two, and another three. This way they brought back meat.

They started out in another direction. I killed two bucks. From there we brought back a large amount of meat. From there we moved camp to the lakes and went out hunting in different directions. Some brought back antelope and some brought back deer. We dried much meat and packed it in parfleches. Coming back with it we camped at Rio Bonito.

70. The Mescalero Beg for Meat

Some of the Jicarilla were camped at Ruidosa with the Mescalero. A number of us started off camping after deer. At the end of the ridge, below on the plains, there were many deer. We established our camp there to hunt deer and antelope. We went off in different directions, hunting, and brought back meat. They brought back white-tailed deer. We killed many animals and dried the meat which we placed in parfleches. We went back with it to Ruidosa.

Again, after that seven men went on horseback south to Tseîntc'îcî, "rock nose". There were many elk tracks there and many of both kinds of deer. We killed a great many and brought home the meat. When we came back among the Mescalero they kept asking us for meat which we gave them. They made a line all the way to our tent. We gave meat to them. When we got back to the tipi with the meat, they ceased asking for it.

Information Concerning Industries and Ceremonies

71. The Sinew-Backed Bow

A piece of wood of which the bow is to be made is cut off the proper length and shaved into shape. Then wide yucca leaves are split from side to side and placed on both sides of the bow in the middle. When it is well covered and wrapped around with these leaves the middle portion is covered with ashes and allowed to remain until it is quite hot. It is then removed, one foot is placed upon the middle of the bow and the two ends are bent back.

A piece of rawhide is placed in the fire and scorched. The rawhide is cut in small pieces and placed in a pot of water which is allowed to boil for a day. Sinew, after being soaked in cold water, is shredded into fine strands. The back of the bow is roughened with a coarse stone. The glue which results from the boiling of the rawhide is then applied. The sinew is wrapped around a long pole and allowed to dry in that position. The glue which has already been applied to the back of the bow is softened by rubbing it with water. The prepared sinew is then applied and the finished bow placed in the sun to dry. When it is dry it is provided with a string. This way they make them.

72. Making the Tipi

When the buffalo hides have been scraped they rub brains on them and work them until they are soft. Seven skins are prepared in this manner, and spread on the ground to dry. The skins are arranged on the ground to form the cover, one entire skin being placed in such a position as to form the back. Much sinew having been prepared for thread by twisting, many women assemble and assist in the sewing. When the skins have been sewed together they are placed in water. The tipi poles are then set up. The tipi cover having been attached to the pole which is to stand at the back, many women take hold of it. As they do this, one of them whistles. They pull the cover from both sides toward the center, saying, "Make it lap." They put in above the doorway the sticks which have been cut the proper length. The cover is fastened to the ground around the bottom by means of pegs. The two poles are inserted to hold the flaps at the smoke hole called its mouth. Finally, they dig a place for the fire.

While the others are sitting about, the medicineman takes a firedrill and starts the fire. The women prepare food for a feast and when it is evening the people gather. About dark, the medicineman begins to sing and continues with the assistance of the others until dawn. They eat about midnight and again in the morning.

The sinew which is left from the sewing is tied with eagle down to the inside of the tipi. This is the way tipis are made.

They used to live in it as in a house. Even during the winter the cold did not penetrate. When the cover of the tipi became hard they worked it again between their hands until it was soft. When camp was moved, it was nicely folded and packed on a horse. In this manner they moved it about.

73. Methods of Cooking Corn

In olden times corn was roasted in the car and afterward ground with a metate. The meal was stirred into a pot of hot water. When cooked it was removed from the fire and served to the company in bowls. It was eaten from the hand.

Sometimes corn was ground without first being roasted. Wheat, after it had been allowed to sprout, was ground. This with the corn meal was stirred into a large pot and cooked. The corn meal was first stirred in. The pot was then withdrawn from the fire and the ground wheat thoroughly stirred in. It was then placed in the fire and cooked for some time. When it was dished out for serving, sugar was added. They ate it that way, sweetened.

Corn was sometimes cooked in water as mush. It was then poured into a dish-like hollow made in the snow. Sometimes the mush was poured on top of the metate. As it ran off the stone they would say to it, "Run far off from the stone." Then the mush did not run very far from the stone when it was so told. It was eaten with the hands. That way they ate it. Sometimes peas and corn were mixed and cooked with the feet of deer in a pot. When it was boiled they ate it.

Others roasted the peas and then ground them. The meal was placed in water and made into soup. That they ate.

Sometimes wheat flour was kneaded, spread out each way and twisted. This was buried in the ashes. The dried amole fruit was well worked up with the hands in water. When it was soft it was taken out and placed in the ashes. It is called LînîLî.

Some people roasted beans; these were cooked in a pot, and mush not very thick made of them. With this soup they ate bread.

74. The Making of Tiswin

A large quantity of corn is shelled. This is placed in a can with water until it is soaked. The corn is spread on a blanket until it is sprouted. It is placed in the sun until it is dry and then it is ground on the metate. Water is heated in a can by the fire and the meal is stirred in. When the water is about half boiled away the can is refilled. The fluid is strained and allowed to cool. It is poured into a barrel where it stands until it sends up bubbles. When it stops bubbling they drink it.

75. Origin of The Medicine Ceremony

Black Bear, Turkey, Rattlesnake, and all the animals living upon the earth who are in charge of the various fruits came together in one place. They celebrated the medicine dance for the benefit of three sick men.

Having made the fence about the dancing grounds, they spread a buffalo hide over a basket in the back of the tipi where a hole had been dug. They took the moccasins of the three sick men and tied them together. With these they beat upon the basket which had been turned over the hole in the back of the tent and covered with a buffalo hide. The singer uses a rattle made from buffalo tail and the tails of rattlesnakes. While a strong man is beating on the basket with the moccasins, the singer shakes the rattles and sings. This is done for four nights.

A long time ago a ceremony of this sort was held this side (west) of Taos where the mountains stand near each other. The fence was built of brush through which no one is allowed to look from the outside. Someone beat with the moccasins and the others danced. When this part of the ceremony was over a noise was made by rubbing the leg bone of a mountain sheep along a notched stick. The tc'actcini and ts'anat'î [1] came in twice where they were rubbing sticks. They danced until morning. The masked men put corn, cherries and the seed of the amole into a hole in the ground. They also put the tail of a rabbit in a clay pot. When they came in the fourth time the amole and cherries were ripe and the corn was already hard. Where they had thrown the rabbit's tail in the pot a live rabbit jumped out. One of them cut an arrow across and they shot another with it without killing him.

The men who looked through the fence that had been built turned into pine trees. Those standing on the other side who had looked through the fence also became pine trees. For that reason one must not look from the outside through the corral fence in which the medicineman is singing. Of the mountains that stand there the first one is named Nîsdjat'ôhî, and then Isaihî Lîbîgahî "horse's house", L'ôkenkelehi. [2]

[1] There are four tc'actcini who have their bodies including their legs, arms and faces, painted with horizontal black stripes on a background of white clay. Their hair is worn projecting from the sides of their heads like horns. The ts'anat'î, usually twelve in number, have their bodies and faces covered with white clay. They wear bands of yucca leaves about their necks, waists, elbows, wrists, knees, and ankles. They have two eagle feathers in their hair. Neither of them wear masks as do the Navajo.

[2] Forty-eight mountains are mentioned in song. Most of them are named in the text, p. 177.

76. Magic at a Medicine Ceremony

On the west side of the Rio Grande opposite Taos two old men held a ceremony. I was a spectator. The two old men conducted the ceremony for two persons. They put corn in a deep hole and made it grow. They introduced tc'actcînî and ts'anat'î (painted dancers). The ts'anat'î had mullers in their hands. They gave each of the ts'anat'î and the tc'actcînî four ears of corn. Then a large fire was built. The enclosure had been built near the river. They put the musk stirrers in the pot.

When the dancers came in here by the door, they put the corn which they had in their hands in the pot. They put the pot some way from the fire where it did not get hot. They poked in the pot with a stick and there was a crackling noise inside, and smoke came out of it. They danced around the fire four times. The pot was filled with corn. They stood in a row and began to dance. The ts'anat'î stood in front holding the mullers. Corn commenced to grow and put out leaves. When they stopped dancing they held up the mullers to the east, south, west, and north. They broke a muller in two and made it just like one again. They took corn out too. They danced on both sides, carrying the stones.

Then they carried the pot which was filled with corn behind them. They made the people stand in a line and threw the corn to them. There was no corn left in the pot. The people picked up the corn. It was not cooked.

The ts'anat'î went to their tipi and came back. The mullers had become bread. They broke them up and when they came in again they distributed it to the people. They made medicine good for all. That way they made the corn grow up. The ts'anat'î distributed it to the tc'actcînî who ate it.

77. The Tcactcini

Long ago they lived at Tseyakînehî where everything grew. Then they started to war eastward on the plains. From there, they brought home an enemy's scalp. They danced the victory dance. They dug a hole for cooking corn. They built a big fire in the pit and placed corn in it to cook. They danced in the evening and made tc'actcînî, who drove all the girls to the dancing place. After they had danced, one girl was still found at the fireplace. They tried in vain to drive her to the dance. One of the tc'actcînî jumped into the pit and was burned. The other tc'actcînî looked everywhere for him in vain.

A man ran off toward the east looking for him, others to the south, west, and north. They all came back to the dancing place without having found him. They called on all the supernatural ones on the earth to help them. The man went again to the east. They dug a hole for the girl, put her in it, and put a flat stone on top, covering it with ashes. The messenger came back from under the sunrise accompanied by XastcînyaLkîdn, the talking god. From the south came back XastcînyaLgayî, the white god. The messenger went again and came back from under the sunset with XastcînîLtsôyî, the yellow god. The messenger went to the north and came back with Xastcîndîsôsî, the variegated god.

They commenced to look for the lost brother. Eagle down was placed on the top of a stick. With this they went around looking everywhere. When they came above the fire pit all the feathers pointed toward it. "Your brother-in-law is right here," said one of the gods. They all turned their ears to the ground. "Here is our brother-in-law," they said. They could hear the one who had been burned laughing.

Then they commenced to look for the girl. They looked in vain until they came near her and then the feathers all pointed toward her. "There she is," said the leader. Then XastcînyaLkîdn stood with his flint sword facing in four directions in turn. When he faced the direction in which the girl was, he made motions as if to strike her four times. Then when he drew back his sword from the top of her head, he pulled her out from the ground also.

78. The Medicine Ceremony

They spread out sand making it smooth. Around the border of this they put up eagle tail feathers in a circle. The people sit around. They make red, yellow, and white paint. They provide too L'ectcîc, and pollen and blue (made by mixing white paint with charcoal). Here in the center is placed a clay vessel containing water. One person sits on one side and another on this side. They strew down the colors making all the animals which are on the earth. Those sitting around do not omit any of them. They watch the work and ask each other if all have been made. Then those for whom the ceremony is held come there and sit in a row. They sit on all of the animals. The medicineman shakes the rattle and sings. The patients cry very hard. Their hands begin to twist, their feet to get crooked. They cry and their noses run. The medicineman puts the rattle under their feet, on their hands. He embraces them. Now they get well. They drink the medicine and put it all over their bodies. They get well.

79. The Medicine Ceremony (Second Description)

When the medicine ceremony is to be held they first make a lodge. In the lodge they make the sand pictures. Two men go in and make every kind of animal. He pounds the herb. He rolls around like a grizzly and says "wa". The one who has supernatural power for this makes the patient well again.

They also make the tc'actcînî and the ts'anat'î. They dance four nights, the women and the men dancing together as they like. "You shall not discontinue it as long as the world stands," he said. "That is why you shall dance just four nights."

They make cherries and yuccas at the dance (by supernatural power?). They make rabbits too. They make bread. They put mush in a pot and it becomes full. They put it at one side and in one night it is finished. The tc'actcînî have peas for their food. They use dog manure for butter on their bread.

Then they are satisfied. They dance four nights and are happy. This is the way they do when they have the fiesta, the grizzly dance.

80. The Adolescence Ceremony

They come to the holy girl early in the morning. When she is thus holy she becomes YoLkaiîsdzan. They also seek out a young boy and bring him there. An old man comes also. From different directions a number of old women come together who sit about and pray. Sitting outside they smoke and pray for the girl, Isdzannadlecî, saying, "May you be renewed. May I live happily. With strewed pollen may I live happily. This boy, too, Kûbatcîstcîne, may he become new. May I be well. May I live to old age. With strewed L'ectcîc, may I live to old age. May the pollen be on top of my feet."

The boy and girl sit this way back of the fire in the tipi; the girl on the south, the boy on the north side. The clothes with which they are to be dressed are placed in front. The priest sprinkles them with L'ectcîc and pollen. For the girl, there are moccasins, leggings, shirt, beads, bracelets, earrings, feathers, and yellow paint. For the boy, Kûbatcîstcîne, there are moccasins, leggings, shirt, feathers, arrows, quiver, and white paint. The priest puts her moccasins on the girl; he dresses her with her tough moccasins; he puts on her tough leggings; he puts on her tough shirt; he puts on her hard beads; he ties the tough feathers to the crown of her head; he puts about her shoulders the tough buckskin; and then paints her face yellow. He puts on the boy; tough moccasins, tough leggings, tough shirt, hard beads. He ties to his crown tough feathers and places across his breast the carrying strap of the quiver, and then paints his face white. The priest goes out with both of them toward the east. He has in his hand pollen and L'ectcîc. As the sun comes up he strews these toward it. Having strewed them out a little ways he strews more, forming the are of a circle. A little beyond he makes another are of a circle and beyond that another and still another. One of the women stands in front of the tent and calls out "Ready." The girl with the boy behind her runs forward a little way and then turns back. The woman whistles into the girl's mouth. Again, they run forward and turn back, the woman whistling into her mouth again. They run forward again and then turn back. The woman whistles in her mouth. Still again, they run forward, turn back, and the woman whistles in her mouth. They then return to the tent.

Outside the tent there is a pile of corn about so large (two bushels). The girl takes a horn spoon and distributes this among all the women.

Then the boy runs off this way (to the east), pulls out some grass, picks up horse manure and holding it in his hand, returns. He puts them down back of the fire in the tent. Next he runs to the south and returns in the same manner, putting the articles down back of the fire. He goes outside again and runs toward the west, returning from that direction in the same manner and puts the materials behind the fire. He goes out again and runs toward the north. He returns from that direction with the same articles and places them behind the fire.

The old man addresses him saying, "My grandson, you should practice herding horses on foot. Having roped a good horse, you will put your hand on him, saying, 'This sort, my horses will be, very fat. They will like me. They will not become poor. All sorts of property will like me.'" Thus the priest prays. At evening, the women prepare food. The priest comes again, smokes and prays. Other men also come into the tipi and smoking, pray for what they happen to need. The priest begins the singing and continues until the middle of the night. The boy and girl dance side by side back of the fire. All in attendance eat and then return home. The next day about noon, the people come again to eat and then return. In the evening, many people come there. The old man comes also, smokes and prays. The other men also, smoke and pray. The old man commences to sing, stopping about midnight. The people eat and return home in the morning. Many people come at noon for a meal and return home. In the evening, the old man comes again and many people gather outside. The old man smokes and prays and other men also smoke and pray. The old man sings until the middle of the night when they all eat and return home. The next day they return and spend the entire day eating. The old man returns in the evening, smokes and prays. Other men also come into the tipi, smoke and pray. The old man sings and all drink tiswin. There is dancing outside the tipi as well as within. The dancing and eating is continued until morning. At dawn, the priest unties the feathers from the heads of the boy and girl and takes them off. Their hair is washed with amole. He rubs red paint on the cheeks of the boy and girl and puts pollen on the crowns of their heads. He makes a cross, with L'ectcîc on their foreheads and in the center of their cheeks on both sides and also on their chins. The priest paints the faces of all the men and women present with red. Then it is over and they go home.

81. Observances in Butchering Buffalo

When a buffalo is skinned the hide is cut along the shoulder on the right side. The fore leg and shoulder is taken off by cutting under. A piece so long (ten inches) of yellow meat lying along the back is cut off, and thrown toward the east. That piece is not carried home. The biceps muscle is also cut off from both sides of the animal. These pieces also are not carried home. All the remainder of the animal is used. This is the way they do.

"Do not throw the feet about," they are always told, "for it is dangerous." One must not throw about the saddle used upon the horse in bringing in the meat. Nor must the saddle blanket nor the rope nor the bridle be thrown around. If these things are thrown about, the horse may slip and fall. This is the rule. That is all.

82. Ceremony for Buffalo

They bring the medicineman buffalo manure. He makes a level place on the ground. The men being called, come together. Then he scatters down some pollen and strews L'ectcîc toward it and prays. He sings four times and then stops. From over there the buffalo bellow. The buffalo manure stands on edge and moves itself and shakes off the L'ectcîc. All the people believe it is true and pray, saying, "May the buffalo be near us. May we camp there among them. May there be much there to eat. With plenty of meat may we move our camp back to our own country."

This is the way they do when there are no buffalo. From there they go back, carrying the meat with them to their own country. This is the way they do.

83. Prayer for Buffalo

"That the buffalo may be near. I make a smoke for you. There will be many buffalo close to us. You will come close around us. Right there we will go among them and will kill many. There will be much meat, not far from us. We will camp among them, and from there will bring home the meat to our own country," they say.

They sing for the buffalo. "Buffalo are running," they say. They sing. They dance, making horns on each side of their heads. Those who dance make motions. "Hwô" they say. That is the way they sing.

They sing for the young yellow calf also. That is all.

84. Note on Killing Eagles

If one does not know how he does not touch them. He will get sick. His arms and legs will draw up. He can not walk and it causes his bones to ache.

85. Ceremony for An Infant

A vessel of water is placed on the ground in the tipi. The person performing the ceremony standing on the west side of it strews pollen and L'ectcîc toward the dish of water. Both of these powders are also placed on the crown of the baby's head. Water is rubbed on the baby's feet and hands and then it is given a complete bath and its face washed also. The child's face is painted red as is also the string with which it is tied and its blanket. The baby is then wrapped in the blanket which is held in place by the string wound around it. This is the way they do.

86. Avoidance of the Mother-In-Law

The woman was afraid of deer raiser, the man who floated down. It is their custom to be afraid of each other. When a man becomes a woman's son-in-law she is afraid of him. The man also is afraid of his mother-in-law. He does not go close to her. If a man happens to talk to his brother-in-law he feels good about it. That is why it is good that way, he said.

87. The Burial of the Dead

In olden times when anyone died they put on his moccasins, and leggings. If he had many relatives they brought from different places, personal property, such as shirts, leggings, blankets. With these, which were all of the best, they dressed the body. Many people came together and wailed. They painted the face red. The better and smaller pieces of property were placed inside the blanket in which the body was wrapped. The corpse was then placed on a horse which was led by two of his kinsmen. A third man accompanied them. A grave was dug and the body placed in it. Over the grave were placed sticks and stones. The horse was then killed and its head cut off. All the relatives of the deceased cut their hair. This was the way they did.

www.ingramcontent.com/pod-product-compliance
Lightning Source LLC
Chambersburg PA
CBHW032026040426
42448CB00006B/737